CROCHET GEOMETRY

GEOMETRIC PATTERNS TO FIT AND FLATTER

SHANNON MULLETT-BOWLSBY

LARK
New York

New York

An Imprint of Sterling Publishing
1166 Avenue of the Americas
New York, NY 10036

LARK CRAFTS and the distinctive Lark logo
are registered trademarks of
Sterling Publishing Co., Inc.

ISBN: 978-1-4547-0919-0

Distributed in Canada by Sterling Publishing
c/o Canadian Manda Group, 664 Annette Street
Toronto, Ontario, Canada M6S 2C8
Distributed in the United Kingdom by GMC Distribution Services
Castle Place, 166 High Street, Lewes, East Sussex, England BN7 1XU
Distributed in Australia by Capricorn Link (Australia) Pty. Ltd.
P.O. Box 704, Windsor, NSW 2756, Australia

For information about custom editions, special sales,
and premium and corporate purchases, please
contact Sterling Special Sales at 800-805-5489
or specialsales@sterlingpublishing.com.

Photography and illustrations by Jason Mullett-Bowlsby

Manufactured in China

2   4   6   8   10   9   7   5   3   1

larkcrafts.com

CONTENTS

Introduction IV

Getting Started VIII

Shrugs 1
Sleeve Shrug 3
Cocoon Shrug 9
Wrap Front Shrug 13

Cardigans 17
Five Easy Pieces 19
Shawl Collar Cardigan 29
Half Circle Cardigan 37

Pullovers 43
T-top 45
Circle T-top 51
Rectangles Top 57
Gathered Shoulder Sleeveless Top 63
Cowl Neck Tunic 67

Wraps 71
Split Circle Wrap 73
Mainsail Wrap 85
Two Circles Wrap 91
Macramé Look Vest 97

Special Techniques 102

Acknowledgments 109
Chart Key 110
Cable Chart Key 111
Materials 111
About the Designer and Photographer 112
Index 113

INTRODUCTION

What you hold in your hands is the finale of a journey of creation. It began with the spark of an idea in my brain, continued through the sketching and patterning process, transferred to the gifted hands of sample makers and our finisher, translated to the eye of the photographer, and came to rest with the editors.

On behalf of all of those wonderfully talented people and for myself, I say thank you. Yes, you; the person holding this book. By purchasing this book you make what we love to do possible. You make what I do possible. And for that I am grateful.

Let's have a little chat about this book, *Crochet Geometry*, shall we? I'll start with the most common questions we receive: What inspired you? How did you make this come to life?

Let me see if I can sum it up for you in the context of how I created *Crochet Geometry*.

Simply put, a geometric figure is any set of points on a plane or in space. No, don't glaze over; I'm not about to go into a lengthy discussion of my math hobby. Instead, I will simply say that the designs in this book (indeed, design in general) are a beautiful collaboration between geometry and art. From that collaboration, came *Crochet Geometry*.

Want a little more? Follow along with me . . .

I always begin my design process the same way: by thinking about who is going to wear and make my garments and accessories. How are these designs going to look on the people who wear them? How are those designs going to translate into achievable patterns that are gratifying to make, a joy to wear, and look FAB on the wearer?

When I first sketch my designs, I dream and I dream big. I am always looking for ways to make those design dreams a reality while giving you, the maker, designs that are accessible and fashionable through patterns that are achievable and enjoyable to make. In the end, it doesn't matter how vivid my design dreams are, if you can't wear them and won't make them, then my work is all for naught.

Crochet Geometry is one of the results of this constant pursuit of the perfect collaboration between design dreams and achievable pattern making.

For the designs in *Crochet Geometry*, I was drawn to the style of construction I see prevalent in Japanese fashion design texts. Starting with the simplest of geometric shapes, these texts demonstrate how to morph, drape, and evolve those shapes into everything from everyday wearables to over-the-top fusions of art and fashion.

From that inspiration, I started playing with fundamental geometric shapes—like rectangles, circles, and triangles—and manipulating those simple shapes into patterns for garments and accessories with minimal or even no shaping to achieve fashion looks that are immediately wearable, accessible, and achievable by crocheters.

And, at last, you are holding the results in your hands right now! *Crochet Geometry*: a book of crochet garment and accessory patterns based on the elegant manipulation of geometric shapes.

The designs in this book will appeal to both first-time and experienced garment makers alike by combining easily made shapes with exciting texture and lace stitch patterns. The simple shapes compel those of you who are newer stitchers to continue onward and interesting stitch patterns promise to keep experienced stitchers engaged and intrigued.

Easy assembly makes these designs perfect gateway garment pieces for stitchers who have previously only made scarves and afghans while giving experienced garment makers a fun and satisfying experience that keeps them excited and stitching far into the night. Just one more row!

If you are a first-time garment maker, *Crochet Geometry* provides you with a gateway from making afghans and scarves to creating more complex garments and accessories while using many techniques you probably are familiar with and are comfortable with.

If you are an experienced garment maker, *Crochet Geometry* provides you with designs that are intriguing and patterns that offer a challenge to the standard designs found in crochet garments.

The bottom line is this: whether this is your first or your hundredth garment, you will appreciate the use of simple shapes that create powerful visual impact through texture and lace. Finally, there's the bonus benefit—brag-worthy results when you show off your finished work.

But before we get to the showing-off stage, let me point out some of the features of this book.

To help ensure your success with your finished projects, the designs in *Crochet Geometry* were created with you, the maker, in mind and are presented in the "See it. Read it. Make it. Wear it!" style:

SEE IT

These designs are photographed in such a way that real women in various shapes and sizes can see themselves wearing them right away. For this book, we created all samples in size small and selected samples in size 3X. You can see that when we say our patterns fit and flatter sizes small through 5X, we really mean it!

READ IT

The patterns are written in clear language with the mind-set that I am working side by side with you. We have included tips and techniques we use every day in our own studio to help make sure you have the best possible chance of completing a gorgeous project. From the pattern notes at the beginning of each pattern, to little hints and tips throughout, to the tutorial section of this book, we have worked to present these patterns in clear, concise language with definitions and help where you might need it.

MAKE IT

It doesn't matter how pretty a picture is or how much you want to make a project, if you don't have enough information to help you finish successfully, you're never going to get to that showing-off phase we talked about earlier. To that end, we have worked hard to make sure you have all the information you need to complete your project successfully.

First, we included a comprehensive section of written and photo tutorials for more advanced stitches and techniques. These cover everything from the Knotless Starting Chain to finishing techniques like the Locking Mattress Stitch for flawless seams and the End Cap Finishing Stitch for polished fabrics. These are some of the same tutorials that are featured in our most popular classes, and we include them here so you have the best chance at success for completing your project.

Next, each pattern includes instructions for working a fabric swatch to help you not only test your gauge but also to help you learn or brush up on any skills you might need for that particular project. In the Pattern Stitch section, you will see the number of stitches and rows that I worked for each swatch as well as the line-by-line instructions for making the swatch. Techniques and stitches used to make your swatch as well as the blocked gauge you should achieve after blocking your swatch, are all right here at your fingertips. Finally, schematics, assembly diagrams, stitch charts, and notes are included in each pattern where applicable. These four elements are the visual representations of the actual stitching you are doing when you make a garment from this book. Let me tell you a little about each of them and how you can use them.

1. Schematics are those line drawings that look kind of like building blueprints or a sewing pattern. Schematics give you the blocked dimensions for the individual pieces you are making for your garment. They are also an invaluable tool should you wish to alter one of the measurements in the garment you are making to create a more customized fit for your body.

2. Assembly diagrams are very much like schematics and are used with schematics to show you exactly how to put together some of the designs where a picture might work better than words alone. A particularly useful example of an assembly diagram is in the Cocoon Shrug pattern (p. 9), where folding points together is a simple idea that becomes clearer with a visual cue.

3. Stitch charts are one of my favorite tools in patterning—both in writing and making. Stitch charts are those things that look like a cross between the stitches you are making with your hook and something from the walls of a pyramid. Indeed, stitch charts are the visual representation of the stitches you are making and provide another visible cue for creating stitches beyond the words of the written pattern. Be sure to reference your Chart Key and Cable Chart Key (p. 110–111) for an interpretation of each symbol and use these symbols in combination with your written pattern and the project photos.

4. Finally, throughout the pattern text are notes, special points to be mindful of while making your project. These might include hints about where to insert your hook when instructed to work in a stitch two rows below or what to keep in mind when reading the pattern. These notes are often the notes I make to myself in the margins of a pattern as I am writing it. I include the most helpful ones here to give you as much information as possible.

WEAR IT

And now we've arrived at the best part of a project. You're all finished with the stitching, the blocking, the finishing, and now it's time to wear your creation with pride, and a sense of accomplishment that comes with making something with your own hands. Congratulations! You have a skill that everyone wishes they had: You are a maker! Now, put on that creation and know that you look amazing!

So there you have it! You hold in your hands the culmination of the thoughtful work of many talented people who have come together to create this book. From the very first glimmer of an idea in my brain to the editors, sample makers, and photographer, we have all worked together to create this book with you in mind.

I have created designs I know you will be proud to wear and will look FAB in, and our team has worked to ensure each design is presented to you so you have the tools needed to complete your project.

This is a book of very special designs, from graphic stitches to luscious fabrics, to unique constructions. Look into the designs and even into the patterns themselves and see if you recognize the strong influence of the geometric shapes and how they have transformed into *Crochet Geometry*. I hope you enjoy making each of these projects as much as I enjoyed designing them for you.

Stitch On!

GETTING STARTED

So now that you understand some of the background behind what we've created here and you know what to expect inside these pages, you're ready to get started on your first project! Before you take that plunge, let me present you with a few questions to ask yourself to help you pick the right project, and the right yarn, and what techniques and skills you will need to complete a flawless project.

WHICH PROJECT IS RIGHT FOR YOU?

I've made a special point of ensuring there is something for every body and for stitchers of every experience level in this book. Personal taste and style preferences aside, here are some guides we have included regarding those skill levels.

Easy

You have a solid grasp of basic crochet skills like making single, double, half double, and chains, and you have probably made projects like afghans, wraps, and scarves, but this is likely one of your first garments.

Since all of the patterns in *Crochet Geometry* have very easy shaping or no shaping at all, you will find most of these projects will fit your needs. The real key to look for here is the stitch patterns. As with pieces like the Mainsail Wrap Cardi, the garment itself is simple with no seams to sew, but it is the stitch pattern that is the real challenge and why those patterns have a more experienced designation on them.

Patterns marked as Easy are the perfect gateway project for making a first garment. Novice crocheters will have a finished item they will be thrilled to show off while more experienced crocheters will find these patterns to be a great way to sate that hunger for a quick project that results in a beautiful garment in a relatively short period of time.

Intermediate

You are comfortable working with more complicated stitches like lace patterns and basic cables and you've probably made a garment before. Patterns with an Intermediate designation will have some shaping and more complex stitches and finishing. If you have made only a few garments before, you will enjoy the construction and stitch work in these patterns and welcome the challenge of these unique pieces. More experienced garment makers and stitch makers will have no trouble completing these projects and will still be able to amaze others with their stitching skills.

Experienced

You have crochet skills that include complex stitches involving longer lace stitch repeats and complex cable work. You've made garments before and don't shy away from setting in sleeves or assembly of multiple pieces for the joy of a finished project.

Patterns with the Experienced designation have more intricate stitch patterns and require a little more concentration when it comes to making lace stitches and cables.

Crocheters with garment-making experience will find these special stitches a welcome challenge and will love the unique construction of each piece. Even crocheters with less experience can use the elements in these patterns to improve or brush up on their skills and, with a little time spent stitching and a little patience, will have a garment they can feel proud to say they made with their own hands.

HOW DO YOU PICK THE RIGHT YARN FOR YOUR PROJECT?

The part of the design process that takes me the longest and is, to my mind, the most important is the swatching. You see, as a crochet and knitwear designer, I have the unique ability to create custom fabrics for each of my designs. This offers both a blessing and a curse, since the possible combinations of stitches and yarns with different fiber content are endless. I love this process of trying different combinations to produce varying fabrics to the point that surfaces in my studio are often well hidden under piles of swatches sorted by stitch pattern and yarn size or content.

Why do I do this much swatching and testing? So that each of these special creations in *Crochet Geometry* are made from fabrics that perfectly match what the design is supposed to be. In short, I do the work creating the perfect fabric so you don't have to.

Now, I know there are a lot of perfectly valid reasons you might not want to or be able to use the exact yarn I used to create the samples in *Crochet Geometry*. So then what? How do you substitute yarn so you get the same fabric I had in mind when I created these designs? In the patterns, we have provided all the information you need to pick a yarn. Let's take a look at that information now.

Yarn Weight

Below is the Craft Yarn Council's Standard Yarn Weight System chart. In each of the patterns in this book, there is a Materials and Tools section and in it you will see a symbol just like those found in this chart. Each weight of yarn has its own designation based on the size of the yarn.

For example, take a look at the Sleeve Shrug (p. 3) pattern and you will see the pattern has a CYC 3 symbol in the Materials and Tools section. According to the chart, that's a light yarn also known as a DK or light worsted yarn. With this information, you can go online or scurry on over to your favorite place to shop, and buy yarns that have the CYC 3 designation on the ball band or look for yarns that are DK or light worsted-weight yarns.

Yarn Content

What a yarn is made up of is just as vital to the success of your project as the size of the yarn. Using a fuzzy, wooly, fingering-weight yarn will never produce the same drape and next-to-skin softness as the bamboo, wool, and silk blend of the fingering-weight yarn I used in the Wrap Front Shrug (p. 13). Yes, the CYC designations match, but they won't create the same fabric. You wouldn't go into a fabric store and buy linen to make a ball gown. Right? Right. When choosing a yarn to substitute, be sure to pick a yarn that has the same or very similar content if you want to create the same fabric I did here in this book.

CYC Standard Yarn Weight System Chart

	SUPER FINE **1** SUPER FIN Super Fino	FINE **2** FIN Fino	LIGHT **3** LÉGER Ligero	MEDIUM **4** MOYEN Medio
Recommended Metric Hook Size	2.25–3.5 mm	3.5–4.5 mm	4.5–5.5 mm	5.5–6.5 mm
Recommended US Hook Size	B-1 to E-4	E-4 to 7	7 to I-9	I-9 to K-10.5

Blocked Gauge

There is one last test you must put your yarn through before deciding if it will create the fabric you are looking for in your finished project: swatching. Yes, you must make a swatch in order to have absolutely definitive proof that your substitute yarn will work. Making a swatch with your hook and yarn, then blocking that swatch to the Blocked Gauge measurements given in each pattern will tell you whether or not you will be able to make the same fabric.

Let me back up here a bit. Blocked gauge or tension (depending on what part of the world you are in) is that number in the pattern that tells you how many stitches and how many rows you must work in order to make the pattern as it is written. You are already going to make a swatch and block that swatch to know if you are achieving the correct stitches and rows per inch . . . at least you are if you want your finished garment to fit! But here you are going to make a swatch to test your fabric if you are making a yarn substitution. You need to know if your fabric is going to move and drape as I intended it to in my pattern, and your blocked gauge swatch is the perfect way to find out.

To this end, we included information on how to make the swatches for the main pattern stitches in each project. Check the Blocked Gauge section as well as the Pattern Stitch section of the pattern and look for the Swatch information under the name of the pattern stitch. There, you'll find the number of rows and stitches I used to make my swatch. Simply follow the Pattern Stitch instructions, block your swatch to the Blocked Gauge measurements, and see if your stitches match my stitches and if your fabric matches my fabric. It really is a fun process and you have an excuse to buy more yarn to sample!

So here we are at the bottom line again: You are about to invest your time, love, and money into making this project. You should spend time making sure you pick yarn that will give you a finished project you are proud of and feel good wearing! Take a little time to pick your yarn considering the weight and content, then give the yarn a test run with the swatch information in the pattern. You'll be glad you did when you are wearing your finished garment and lookin' amazing in it!

A FEW FINAL WORDS FROM ME BEFORE YOU BEGIN . . .

Making a Gauge Swatch

I already addressed making a blocked gauge swatch in the section about how to pick the right yarn for your project. I want to touch on this again because it is vital to the success of your project.

Achieving the correct blocked stitch and row gauge is how you know your finished garment will fit properly. What you are looking for is if your stitches and rows per inch match the stitches and rows per inch I used to write that particular pattern. Notice that we give the Blocked Gauge for the projects in this book. This means you will make, then block your swatch to obtain the needed stitches and rows per inch. This also means you will stitch slightly tighter than the blocked gauge states. If you stitch to the blocked gauge, your fabric will not open up correctly and will probably sag when wearing.

The process of swatching is fun and relatively short compared to how long it will take you to make your project. Simply look for the Swatch information under the Pattern Stitch section of your pattern. There, I've given the number of rows and stitches I used to make the swatch I used to create my fabric. After you have made your swatch, use your favorite blocking method (spritzing, soaking, steaming) and pin out your swatch to the measurements given in the Blocked Gauge section of the pattern. Now, wait for your swatch to dry, remove the pins, and see if your stitches and rows match my stitches and rows. If so, you're ready to go! If not, no worries—make another swatch, adjusting your stitching tension either tighter or looser depending on your blocked results.

Swatching is one of the most important steps in my design process. For me, making a swatch is how I choose the stitches and yarn I use to create the best fabric for my design, and it is how I know how many stitches and rows per inch to use to write my pattern so you can make my design for yourself. For you, making a swatch is how you choose your yarn and confirm you are making the correct fabric for your project, and how you know if you are matching the pattern stitches and rows per inch so your finished project is a success. There's that bottom line again: Swatching is fun and creative and is more than worth the time and effort to ensure you finish with a FAB project!

A WORD (OR TWO) ABOUT BLOCKING

Just do it. Okay . . . that was three words. There are two places in every pattern where blocking plays an important role in the process of making. The first place is at the beginning of the process where we are making a blocked swatch as we just finished discussing in the previous section. The second place is at or near the end of the process of making our project. Here, the instructions will read "Block all pieces to measurements in schematic." Just as with your swatch, you will use the appropriate method of introducing moisture to your finished fabric (spritzing, soaking, or steaming), then gently shape those fabric pieces into the dimensions given in the schematic. Pin the pieces into place and let them dry to their final shape.

Why should you do this? I could go on about this for pages and pages, but I suspect my editor wouldn't look upon that very kindly since this is a book of patterns and not a treatise on the joys and benefits of blocking. So I will compress my thoughts here:

Benefits

1. Blocking the fabric pieces sets the fabric into its final shape. This makes the garment fit properly and, if you are sewing pieces together, makes the edges straighter for easier sewing.

2. Blocking opens up your stitches, giving them greater clarity and definition. And I'm not just talking about lace work here! Blocking stitches does open up lace beautifully, showing all that skill you put into making it, but block.ing also sets texture and solid stitch patterns into place so they line up properly giving your finished fabric a polished, professional look.

3. Correct blocking techniques allow the fibers in your fabric to be all they can be! Whether you are adding moisture to allow a beautiful wool blend to open up and soften the fibers or if you are steaming an acrylic blend to add softness and drape, proper introduction of water to fibers makes them into beautiful, finished fabrics.

INTERPRETING THE LINGO

There is a lot of "pattern speak" in written crochet patterns that we use in order to save space. Most of you are familiar with these abbreviations like FPdc, sp, st, and ch. However, you might encounter a few that are either new to you or that you might not recognize because you are not from the United States where this pattern was written. Yes, there is a whole different set of pattern speak for crochet patterns in countries other than the United States. To avoid potential confusion, we provide the following interpretation tools.

The first of these tools is the Abbreviations chart (p. XIV). This will act as your key to all of the FPdc, First-dc, and 4/4 FPdtr/trtr stitches throughout this book. If you see something that you aren't sure about, check this chart for confirmation.

The second tool is a US to UK Conversion Table for crochet terminology (p. XIV). This will cover a great

deal of the terms that are different in US crochet patterns versus UK crochet patterns. Most people are familiar with these two methods of writing crochet patterns and can use this chart to convert the patterns in this book, which are written in US crochet terminology to UK terminology.

Finally, the Stitch Guide is the tool you will use to see exactly what we mean when we name a specific stitch in a pattern. For example, your understanding of how many chain stitches are in a Sc-V stitch might be different than I intended in my pattern. And just what is a First-dc stitch? Wanna know? Look it up in the Stitch Guide included in the beginning of every pattern.

There are a lot of sts, chs, sps, and first-dc stitches out there, and we've made sure you have the tools you need to interpret them all without getting tripped up on the lingo of crochet pattern speak.

Abbreviations

1/1	1-over-1	**dtr**	Double treble crochet	**FPsc**	front post single crochet	**sc2tog**	Single crochet 2 together
2/2	2-over-2	**Ext-Fdc**	Extending foundation double crochet	**FPtr**	front post treble crochet	**sc-tbl**	single crochet through back loop
2/3	2-over-3	**Ext-Fsc**	Extending foundation single crochet	**FPtrtr**	front post triple treble crochet	**sc-tfl**	single crochet through front loop
3/3	3-over-3	**ext-sc**	extended single crochet	**Fsc**	foundation single crochet	**Sc-V**	single crochet V-stitch
3-2-3	3-over-2-over-3	**Fdc**	Foundation double crochet	**hdc**	half double crochet	**sk**	skip
BPdc	Back post double crochet	**First-dc**	First-double crochet	**inverted Dc-V**	inverted double crochet V-stitch	**sl st**	slip stitch
ch(s)	chain(s)	**First-dc2tog**	First-double crochet 2 together	**LC**	Left cross cable	**sp(s)**	space(es)
cm	centimeters	**First-tr**	First-treble crochet	**mm**	millimeters	**st(s)**	stitches
dc	double crochet	**FP-Cl**	Front post cluster stitch	**RC**	Right cross cable	**Tr**	Treble crochet
dc2tog	double crochet 2 together	**FPdc**	Front post double crochet	**rep**	repeat	**trtr**	Triple treble crochet
dc3tog	double crochet 3 together	**FPdc-V**	Front post double crochet V-stitch	**rnd(s)**	round(s)	**var**	variation
dc-fan	double crochet-fan	**FPdtr**	front post double treble crochet	**RS**	right side	**WS**	wrong side
Dc-V	Double crochet V-stitch	**FPdtr/trtr**	front post double treble crochet/triple treble crochet	**sc**	single crochet	**yo**	yarn over

US to UK Conversion Table

US Terminology	UK Terminology
single crochet (sc)	Double Crochet (dc)
Half double crochet (hdc)	Half treble (htr)
Double Crochet (dc)	Treble (tr)
Treble (tr)	Double treble (dtr)

US Terminology	UK Terminology
Double treble (dtr)	Triple Treble (trtr)
Skip	Miss
gauge	tension
yarn over (yo)	yarn over hook (yoh)

SHRUGS

SLEEVE SHRUG

Pure simplicity is the basis for this twist on a sleeve shrug. Here, we've taken the rectangle and given it a gentle curve to provide subtle shaping for the sleeves and main body. By working progressively taller and then shorter stitches across the Non-Stick Lace Feather and Fan stitch, we created shaping that you won't even notice you're working. And wait until you block this one. It's all about the stitch pattern, and the Non-Stick Lace Feather and Fan is going to take your breath away.

SKILL LEVEL: ⬤■■■◗
Experienced

SIZES: S/M (L/1X, 2X/3X, 4X/5X)
Sample shown in size small/medium

FINISHED MEASUREMENTS
To Fit Bust: 31–38 (39–46, 47–54, 55–62)"/78.5–96.5 (99–117, 119.5–137, 139.5–157.5) cm
Cuff to Cuff: 57 (60, 65, 68)"/145 (152.5, 165, 172.5) cm

MATERIALS AND TOOLS
 Sample uses Lion Brand Collection, Superwash Merino (100% superwash merino wool; 3.5 ounces/100 g = 306 yards/280 m): 3 (4, 4, 5) balls in color Wild Berry #486-141—918 (1224, 1224, 1530) yards/840 (1120, 1120, 1400) m of lightweight yarn
Crochet hook: 3.75 mm (size F-5) or size to obtain gauge
Yarn needle

BLOCKED GAUGES
Double crochet raised non-stick lace feather and fan: 6 sts = 1"/2.5 cm; 48 sts = 8"/20.5 cm; 2.67 rows = 1"/2.5 cm; 12 rows = 4.5"/11.5 cm
Treble crochet raised non-stick lace feather and fan: 6 sts = 1"/2.5; 48 sts = 8"/20.5 cm; 2.18 rows = 1"/2.5; 12 rows = 5.5"/14 cm
Double treble crochet raised non-stick lace feather and fan: 5.33 sts = 1"/2.5 cm; 48 sts = 9"/23 cm; 1.85 rows = 1"/2.5 cm; 12 rows = 6.5"/16.5 cm

STITCH GUIDE

Foundation single crochet (Fsc): Ch 2, insert hook in 2nd ch from hook, yo and draw up a loop, yo and draw through 1 loop (first "chain" made), yo and draw through 2 loops on hook (first Fsc made), *insert hook under 2 loops of the "chain" just made, yo and draw up a loop, yo and draw through 1 loop ("chain" made), yo and draw through 2 loops on hook (Fsc made); rep from * for indicated number of foundation sts.

Front post single crochet (FPsc): Insert hook from front to back and to front again around the post of the indicated st, yo and draw up a loop, yo and draw through both loops on hook.

First double crochet (First-dc): Sc in first st, ch 2. *Note:* Use this st whenever the first st of a row is a dc. When working back in the First-dc at the end of the following row, insert hook into the second ch of the ch-2.

Treble crochet (tr): Yo twice, insert hook in next st, yo and draw up a loop, (yo and draw through 2 loops on hook) 3 times.

Double treble crochet (dtr): Yo 3 times, insert hook into indicated st, yo and draw up a loop, (yo and draw through 2 loops on hook) 4 times.

First treble crochet (First-tr): Sc in first st, ch 3. *Note:* Use this st whenever the first st of a row is a tr. When working back in the First-tr at the end of the following row, insert hook into the third ch of the ch-3.

PATTERN STITCH

Treble crochet raised non-stick lace feather and fan (tr Raised Non-Stick Lace Feather and Fan) (worked on a multiple of 15 + 3 sts)

Swatch: 48 sts and 12 rows (+1 Fsc row)

Foundation Row: Work 48 Fsc, turn.

Row 1 (RS): First-tr, yo, insert hook in next st, yo and pull up a loop to height of First-tr, [sk next st, insert hook in next st, yo and pull up a loop to height of First-tr] twice (5 loops on hook), yo and draw through 4 loops on hook, yo and draw through remaining 2 loops on hook (sc made), sc 2 times under same 4 loops just worked, sk next st, tr in next st, 4 tr in next st, *4 tr in next st, tr in next st, yo, [sk next st, insert hook into next st, yo and pull up a loop to height of tr] 5 times (7 loops on hook), yo and draw through 6 loops on hook, yo and draw through remaining 2 loops on hook (sc made), sc 4 times under same 6 loops just worked, sk next st, tr in next st, 4 tr in next st; rep from * to last 9 sts, 4 tr in next st, tr in next st, yo, [sk next st, insert hook in next st, yo and pull up a loop to height of tr] 3 times (5 loops on hook), yo and draw through 4 loops on hook, yo and draw through remaining 2 loops on hook (sc made), sc 2 times under same 4 loops just worked, tr in last st, turn.

Row 2: Ch 1, sc in first st, sc in each of next 3 sts, FPsc around each of next 10 sts, *sc in each of next 5 sts, FPsc around each of next 10 sts; rep from * to last 4 sts, sc in each of next 4 sts, turn.

Rep rows 1 and 2 for pattern st.

Treble Crochet Raised Non-Stick Lace Feather and Fan

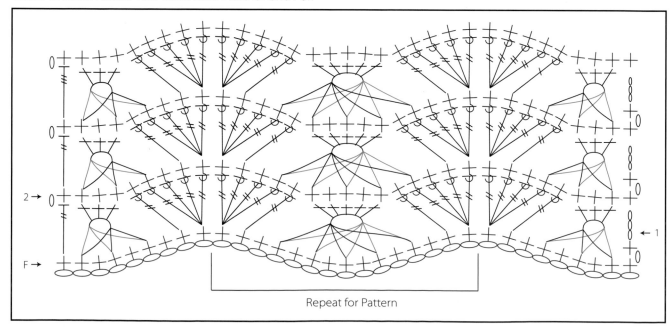

Repeat for Pattern

SPECIAL TECHNIQUES

Knotless Starting Chain (see Special Techniques, p. 103)
End Cap Finishing Stitch (see Special Techniques, p. 108)
Locking Mattress Stitch (see Special Techniques, p. 104)

NOTE

Shrug is made in one piece from the bottom up; shaping is achieved by working progressively shorter stitches toward the sleeve cuffs.

INSTRUCTIONS

Foundation Row: Work 333 (348, 378, 393) Fsc, turn.

Row 1 (RS): First-dc, yo, insert hook in next st, yo and pull up a loop to height of First-dc, [sk next st, insert hook in next st, yo and pull up a loop to height of First-dc] twice (5 loops on hook), yo and draw through 4 loops on hook, yo and draw through remaining 2 loops on hook (sc made), sc 2 times under same 4 loops just worked, sk next st, dc in next st, dc 4 times in next st;

[dc 4 times in next st, dc in next st, yo, (sk next st, insert hook into next st, yo and pull up a loop to height of dc) 5 times (7 loops on hook), yo and draw through 6 loops on hook, yo and draw through remaining 2 loops on hook (sc made), sc 4 times under same 6 loops just worked, sk next st, dc in next st, dc 4 times in next st] 3 (3, 4, 4) times;

[tr 4 times in next st, tr in next st, yo, (sk next st, insert hook into next st, yo and pull up a loop to height of tr) 5 times (7 loops on hook), yo and draw through 6 loops on hook, yo and draw through remaining 2 loops on hook (sc made), sc 4 times under same 6 loops just worked, sk next st, tr in next st, tr 4 times in next st] 5 times;

[dtr 4 times in next st, dtr in next st, yo, (sk next st, insert hook into next st, yo and pull up a loop to height of dtr) 5 times (7 loops on hook), yo and draw through 6 loops on hook, yo and draw through remaining 2 loops on hook (sc made), sc 4 times under same 6 loops just worked, sk next st, dtr in next st, dtr 4 times in next st] 5 (6, 6, 7) times;

[tr 4 times in next st, tr in next st, yo, (sk next st, insert hook into next st, yo and pull up a loop to height of tr) 5 times (7 loops on hook), yo and draw through 6 loops on hook, yo and draw through remaining 2 loops on hook (sc made), sc 4 times under same 6 loops just worked, sk next st, tr in next st, tr 4 times in next st] 5 times;

[dc 4 times in next st, dc in next st, yo, (sk next st, insert hook into next st, yo and pull up a loop to height of dc) 5 times (7 loops on hook), yo and draw through 6 loops on hook, yo and draw through remaining 2 loops on hook (sc made), sc 4 times under same 6 loops just worked, sk next st, dc in next st, dc 4 times in next st] 3 (3, 4, 4) times;

dc 4 times in next st, dc in next st, yo, (sk next st, insert hook in next st, yo and pull up a loop to height of dc) 3 times (5 loops on hook), yo and draw through 4 loops on hook, yo and draw through remaining 2 loops on hook (sc made), sc 2 times under same 6 loops just worked, dc in last st, turn.

Row 2: Work row 2 of tr Raised Non-Stick Lace Feather and Fan pattern st.

Rows 3–26 (28, 30, 30): Rep rows 1 and 2.

Cut yarn, leaving tail for weaving; weave in tail using End Cap Finishing Stitch.

FINISHING

Block all pieces to measurements in schematic.
Fold in half lengthwise according to assembly diagram; using Locking Mattress Stitch, sew sleeve seams, leaving 22.5 (24, 25.5, 26.5)" for main body opening.

NOTE: Sleeve seams can be made longer or shorter for a more custom fit across main body. To ensure best fit, pin sleeve seams, leaving main body opening as designated above for your size and adjust if needed.

Gently block seams to even out.
Weave in all ends.

Sleeve Shrug Schematic and Assembly

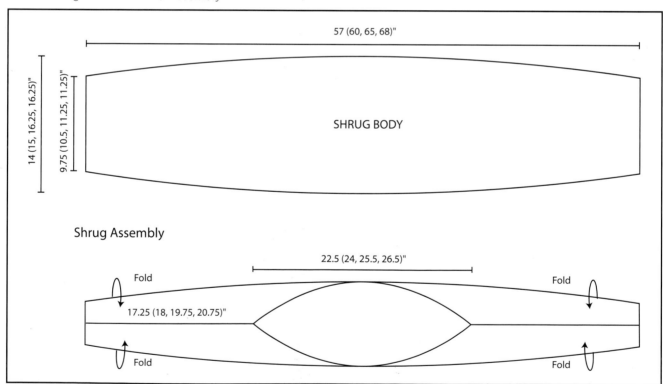

COCOON SHRUG

Here again the humble rectangle is transformed. This time our rectangle's congruent angles are softened and become a dramatic Cocoon Shrug with two easy seams. The plush cable pattern adds a standout textural look, giving this shrug a comfy feel with an upscale look.

SKILL LEVEL: ⬛⬛⬛▭
Intermediate

SIZES: S/M (L/1X, 2X/3X, 4X/5X)
Sample shown in size small/medium

FINISHED MEASUREMENTS
To Fit Bust: 32–39 (40–47, 48–55, 56–63)"/81.5–99 (101.5–119.5, 122–140, 142.5–160) cm
Finished Cuff to Cuff: 34.25 (36.5, 37.75, 39)" /87 (93, 96, 99) cm
Finished Width Top to Bottom: 23 (24.25, 25.25, 26.5)"/58.5 (61.5, 64, 67.5) cm
Armhole Opening: 6 (7, 7.5, 8)"/15 (18, 19, 20) cm

MATERIALS AND TOOLS

Sample uses Lion Brand, Wool-Ease (80% acrylic, 20% wool; 3 ounces/85 g = 197 yards/180 m): 4 (5, 6, 6) skeins in color Cranberry #620-138—788 (985, 1182, 1182) yards/721 (901, 1081, 1081) m of worsted-weight yarn

Crochet hook: 5.00 mm (size H-8) or size to obtain gauge
Yarn needle

BLOCKED GAUGE
Cable: 3.56 sts = 1"/2.5 cm; 32 sts = 9"/23 cm; 1.69 rows = 1"/2.5 cm; 11 rows = 6.5"/16.5 cm

STITCH GUIDE

Foundation double crochet (Fdc): Ch 2, insert hook in 2nd ch from hook, yo and draw up a loop, yo and draw through 1 loop (first "chain" made), yo and draw through 2 loops on hook, ch 2 (first Fdc made), *yo, insert hook under 2 loops of the "chain" just made, yo and draw up a loop, yo and draw through 1 loop ("chain" made), (yo and draw through 2 loops on hook) twice (Fdc made); rep from * for indicated number of foundation sts.

First double crochet (First-dc): Sc in first st, ch 2. *Note:* Use this st whenever the first st of a row is a dc. When working back in the First-dc at the end of the following row, insert hook into the second ch of the ch-2.

Front post double crochet (FPdc): Yo, insert hook from front to back and then to front again around post of indicated st, yo and draw up a loop, [yo and draw through 2 loops on hook] 2 times.

Back post double crochet (BPdc): Yo, insert hook from back to front and then to back again around post of indicated st, yo and draw up a loop, [yo and draw through 2 loops on hook] twice.

Front post double treble crochet (FPdtr): Yo 3 times, insert hook from front to back and then to front again around post of indicated st, yo and draw up a loop, [yo and draw through 2 loops on hook] 4 times.

Front post triple treble crochet (FPtrtr): Yo 4 times, insert hook from front to back and then to front again around post of indicated st, yo and draw up a loop, [yo and draw through 2 loops on hook] 5 times.

4-over-4 front post double treble/triple treble crochet left cross cable (4/4 FPdtr/trtr LC) (worked over 8 sts): Sk next 4 sts, FPdtr around each of next 4 sts; working in front of FPdtr just made, FPtrtr around each of first 4 skipped sts.

Cocoon Shrug Cable

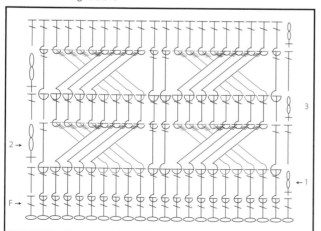

PATTERN STITCH

Cable (worked on a multiple of 10 + 2)

Swatch: 32 sts and 9 rows

Foundation Row: Work 32 Fdc, turn

Row 1: First-dc, FPdc around next st, BPdc around each of next 8 sts, *FPdc around each of next 2 sts, BPdc around each of next 8 sts; rep from * to last 2 sts, FPdc around next st, dc in last st, turn.

Row 2 (RS): First-dc, BPdc around next st, work 4/4 FPdtr/trtr LC, *BPdc around each of next 2 sts, work 4/4 FPdtr/trtr LC; rep from * to last 2 sts, BPdc around next st, dc in last st, turn.

Rep rows 1 and 2 for pattern st.

SPECIAL TECHNIQUES

Knotless Starting Chain (see Special Techniques, p. 103)
End Cap Finishing Stitch (see Special Techniques, p. 108)
Locking Mattress Stitch (see Special Techniques, p. 104)

NOTE

Garment is made in one piece from cuff to cuff, then the sleeve seams are sewn according to finishing instructions.

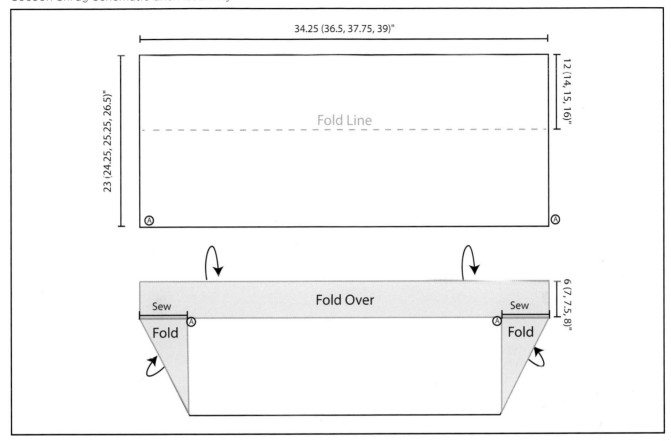

INSTRUCTIONS

Foundation Row: Work 82 (86, 90, 94) Fdc, turn.

Row 1: First-dc, FPdc around each of next 6 (8, 5, 7) sts, BPdc around each of next 8 sts, *FPdc around each of next 2 sts, BPdc around each of next 8 sts; rep from * to last 7 (9, 6, 8) sts, FPdc around each of next 6 (8, 5, 7) sts, dc in last st, turn.

Row 2 (RS): First-dc, BPdc around each of next 6 (8, 5, 7) sts, work 4/4 FPdtr/trtr LC, *BPdc around each of next 2 sts, work 4/4 FPdtr/trtr LC; rep from * to last 7 (9, 6, 8) sts, BPdc around each of next 6 (8, 5, 7) sts, dc in last st, turn.

Rows 3–56 (60, 62, 64): Rep rows 1 and 2.

Row 57 (61, 63, 65): Rep row 1.

Row 58 (62, 64, 66): First-dc, dc in each st to end of row.

Cut yarn, leaving tail for weaving in; pull tail through last st made; weave in using End Cap Finishing Stitch.

FINISHING

Block to measurements in schematic.
Fold and sew seams according to assembly diagram.
Weave in all ends.

WRAP FRONT SHRUG

Sometimes the simplest design makes the most dramatic statement—and this wrap front shrug certainly speaks volumes. This unique accessory combines the best of a shrug with the drama of a wrap. Made from the center out, this pattern is entirely customizable, allowing you to adjust the fit across the back and to lengthen or shorten the front panels. Simple rectangles for the body and wrap, and trapezoids for the sleeves allowed us to really go for it with a geometric mirroring lace pattern. Enjoy making this one, then go out and make a statement of your own!

SKILL LEVEL: ◼◼◼◻
Intermediate

SIZES: S (M, L, XL, 2X, 3X, 4X, 5X)
Sample shown in size small

FINISHED MEASUREMENTS
To Fit Bust: 32 (36, 40, 44, 48, 52, 56, 60)"/81.5 (91.5, 101.5, 112, 122, 132, 142, 152.5) cm
Finished Length from Shoulder: 13 (13, 13.5, 13.5, 14.25, 14.25, 14.75, 14.75)"/33 (33, 34.5, 34.5, 36, 36, 37.5, 37.5) cm

MATERIALS AND TOOLS

Sample uses Crystal Palace Yarns, Panda Silk (52% bamboo, 43% machine-washable merino wool, 5% combed silk; 1.75 ounces/50 g = 204 yards/187 m): 8 (9, 10, 11, 12, 12, 13, 14) balls in color Mars Red #3033—1632 (1836, 2040, 2244, 2448, 2448, 2652, 2856) yards/1493 (1679, 1866, 2052, 2239, 2239, 2425, 2612) m of superfine-weight yarn
Crochet hook: 2.75 mm (size C-2) or size to obtain gauge
Yarn needle

BLOCKED GAUGE
Stacked Lace: 6.83 sts = 1"/2.5 cm; 41 sts = 6"/15 cm; 3.2 rows = 1"/2.5 cm; 21 rows = 6.25"/16 cm

STITCH GUIDE

Foundation single crochet (Fsc): Ch 2, insert hook in 2nd ch from hook, yo and draw up a loop, yo and draw through 1 loop (first "chain" made), yo and draw through 2 loops on hook (first Fsc made), *insert hook under 2 loops of the "chain" just made, yo and draw up a loop, yo and draw through 1 loop ("chain" made), yo and draw through 2 loops on hook (Fsc made); rep from * for indicated number of foundation sts.

First double crochet (First-dc): Sc in first st, ch 2. *Note:* Use this st whenever the first st of a row is a dc. When working back in the First-dc at the end of the following row, insert hook into the second ch of the ch-2.

Double crochet V-stitch (Dc-V): (Dc, ch 2, dc) in indicated st or sp.

3-double crochet fan (3-dc fan): Dc 3 times in indicated st or sp.

Inverted double crochet V-stitch (inverted Dc-V): Yo, insert hook in next ch sp, yo and draw up a loop, yo and draw through 2 loops on hook, sk next st, yo, insert hook in next ch sp, yo and draw up a loop, yo and draw through 2 loops on hook, yo and draw through all 3 loops on hook.

Double crochet 3 together (dc3tog): Yo, insert hook in indicated st or sp, yo and draw up a loop, yo and draw through 2 loops on hook, (yo, insert hook in next st, yo and draw up a loop, yo and draw through 2 loops on hook) twice, yo and draw through all 4 loops on hook.

PATTERN STITCH

Stacked Lace (worked on a multiple of 3 + 2 sts)

Swatch: 41 sts and 20 rows (+1 Fsc row)

Foundation Row: Work 41 Fsc, turn.

Row 1: First-dc, *sk next st, Dc-V in next st, sk next st; rep from * to last st, dc in last st, turn.

Row 2: First-dc, 3-dc fan in ch-2 sp of each Dc-V to last st, dc in last st, turn.

Row 3: First-dc, *ch 1, dc3tog, ch 2; rep from * to last st, dc in last st, turn.

Row 4: First-dc, *ch 1, inverted Dc-V, ch 2; rep from * to last st, dc in last st, turn.

Row 5: Ch 1, sc in first st and in each st and ch to end of row, turn.

Rep rows 1–5 for pattern st.

Stacked Lace

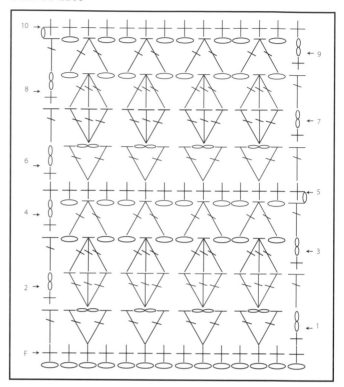

SPECIAL TECHNIQUES

End Cap Finishing Stitch (see Special Techniques, p. 108)
Locking Mattress Stitch (see Special Techniques, p. 104)

NOTES

1. Garment is made from center of Back out to armholes; Front panels are made separately, then sewn to Back, leaving openings for armholes; shoulder seams sewn; sleeves are made separately from top of sleeve down, then sewn to armhole openings.

2. Generally, when instructed to decrease "in pattern stitch as established," you will work the first stitch of the row as in pattern stitch, then work two stitches together, then work the same type of stitch until another repeat of the pattern stitch can be established. For example, if you are working on a row that begins with a double crochet, you would work a double crochet in the first stitch, double crochet two together, then double crochet until you can start another repeat of the 3-stitch pattern repeat of the Stacked Lace pattern stitch. Likewise at the end of a row, you would work in pattern as established, then work double crochet over any partial sections of the 3-stitch pattern repeat of the Stacked Lace pattern stitch, double crochet 2 together, then work a double crochet in the last stitch.

INSTRUCTIONS

Back
First Side
Foundation Row: Work 89 (89, 92, 92, 98, 98, 101, 101) Fsc, turn.

Rows 1–29 (32, 36, 39, 42, 46, 48, 52): Work in Stacked Lace pattern st.

Next Row: Ch 1, sc in first st and in each st and ch to end of row.

Cut yarn, leaving tail for weaving in; pull tail through last st made; weave in tail using End Cap Finishing Stitch.

Second Side
With RS facing, join yarn in first Fsc made; first st of row 1 made in same st as joining.

Rows 1–29 (32, 36, 39, 42, 46, 48, 52): Work in Stacked Lace pattern st.

Next Row: Ch 1, sc in first st and in each st and ch to end of row.

Cut yarn, leaving tail for weaving in; pull tail through last st made; weave in tail using End Cap Finishing Stitch.

Front Panels (make 2)
Foundation Row: Work 89 (89, 92, 92, 98, 98, 101, 101) Fsc, turn.

Rows 1–90 (100, 105, 110, 115, 115, 115, 115): Work in Stacked Lace pattern st.

Sizes S (M, L, 1X, 4X, 5X) Only
Rows 91 (101, 106, 111, 116, 116)–93 (103, 106, 112, 119, 119): Work in Stacked Lace pattern st.

All Sizes
Next Row: Ch 1, sc in first st and in each st and ch to end of row.

Cut yarn, leaving tail for weaving in; pull tail through last st made; weave in tail using End Cap Finishing Stitch.

Sleeve (make 2)
Foundation Row: Work 101 (107, 119, 125, 134, 140, 149, 155) Fsc, turn.

Rows 1–21 (21, 22, 22, 23, 23, 24, 24): Work in Stacked Lace pattern st and decrease as follows:

First decrease 1 st at beginning and end of every 1 (1, 1, 1, 2, 2, 2) rows 11 (15, 8, 6, 5, 10, 6, 6) times—79 (77, 103, 113, 124, 120, 137, 143) sts.

Then decrease 1 st at beginning and end of every 2 (2, 2, 2, 2, 3, 3, 3) rows 5 (3, 7, 8, 9, 1, 4, 4) times—69 (71, 89, 97, 106, 118, 129, 135) sts.

Cut yarn, leaving tail for weaving in; pull tail through last st made; weave in tail using End Cap Finishing Stitch.

FINISHING

Block all pieces to measurements in schematic.
Using Locking Mattress Stitch, sew seams as follows:
Sew Front Panels to Back along shoulder seam leaving 7 (7, 8, 8, 9, 9.5, 10, 10)"/18 (18, 20.5, 20.5, 23, 24, 25.5, 25.5) cm for back neckline.
Sew side seams of main body leaving 7 (7.5, 8, 8.5, 9, 9.5, 10, 10.5)"/18 (19, 20.5, 21.5, 23, 24, 25.5, 26.5) cm for armholes.
Set sleeve into armholes and sew into place.
Sew sleeve seams.
Gently steam block sewn seams, if needed
Weave in all ends.

Wrap Front Shrug Schematic

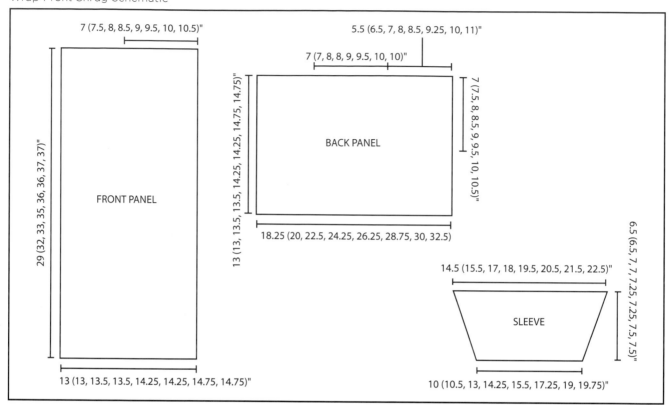

FRONT PANEL

7 (7.5, 8, 8.5, 9, 9.5, 10, 10.5)"

29 (32, 33, 35, 36, 36, 37, 37)"

13 (13, 13.5, 13.5, 14.25, 14.25, 14.75, 14.75)"

BACK PANEL

5.5 (6.5, 7, 8, 8.5, 9.25, 10, 11)"

7 (7, 8, 8, 9, 9.5, 10, 10)"

7 (7.5, 8, 8.5, 9, 9.5, 10, 10.5)"

13 (13, 13.5, 13.5, 14.25, 14.25, 14.75, 14.75)"

18.25 (20, 22.5, 24.25, 26.25, 28.75, 30, 32.5)

SLEEVE

14.5 (15.5, 17, 18, 19.5, 20.5, 21.5, 22.5)"

6.5 (6.5, 7, 7, 7.25, 7.25, 7.5, 7.5)"

10 (10.5, 13, 14.25, 15.5, 17.25, 19, 19.75)"

CARDIGANS

FIVE EASY PIECES

The name says it all! This stunning cardi is made from five easy-to-make pieces: three rectangles and two trapezoids. The simplicity of the main pattern pieces allowed us to lavish all our attention on the pattern stitches. The stunning cables on the center back panel will take your breath away, and the reversible lace pattern made with post stitches is light and airy on one side with dramatic lace ribbing on the other.

SKILL LEVEL: ⬛⬛⬛⬜
Experienced

SIZES: S (M, L, XL, 2X, 3X, 4X, 5X)
Samples shown in size small and 3X

FINISHED MEASUREMENTS

To Fit Bust: 32 (36, 40, 44, 48, 52, 56, 60)"/81.5 (91.5, 101.5, 112, 122, 132, 142, 152.5) cm

Finished Bust: 36 (40, 44, 48, 52, 56, 60, 64)"/91.5 (101.5, 112, 122, 132, 142, 152.5, 162.5) cm

Finished Length from Shoulder: 25.5 (26, 26.5, 27, 27.5, 28, 28.5, 29)"/65 (66, 67.5, 68.5, 70, 71, 72.5, 73.5) cm

MATERIALS AND TOOLS

Sample uses Lion Brand Collection, Superwash Merino (100% superwash merino wool; 3.5 ounces/100 g = 306 yards/280 m): 7 (8, 9, 10, 11, 12, 12, 13) balls; size small shown in color Cayenne #486-144; size 3X shown in color Persimmon #486-135—2142 (2448, 2754, 3060, 3366, 3672, 3672, 3978) yards/1959 (2239, 2519, 2799, 3078, 3358, 3358, 3638) m of lightweight yarn

Crochet hook: 3.75 mm (size F-5) or size to obtain gauge

Yarn needle

BLOCKED GAUGES

Raised front double crochet V-stitch and fans: 4.82 sts = 1"/2.5 cm; 41 sts = 8.5"/21.5 cm; 2.27 rows = 1"/2.5 cm; 17 rows = 7.5"/19 cm

Trellis cable: 4.6 sts = 1"/2.5 cm; 4.62 rows = 1"/2.5 cm

STITCH GUIDE

Foundation single crochet (Fsc): Ch 2, insert hook in 2nd ch from hook, yo and draw up a loop, yo and draw through 1 loop (first "chain" made), yo and draw through 2 loops on hook (first Fsc made), *insert hook under 2 loops of the "chain" just made, yo and draw up a loop, yo and draw through 1 loop ("chain" made), yo and draw through 2 loops on hook (Fsc made); rep from * for indicated number of foundation sts.

Foundation double crochet (Fdc): Ch 2, insert hook in 2nd ch from hook, yo and draw up a loop, yo and draw through 1 loop (first "chain" made), yo and draw through 2 loops on hook, ch 2 (first Fdc made), *yo, insert hook under 2 loops of the "chain" just made, yo and draw up a loop, yo and draw through 1 loop ("chain" made), (yo and draw through 2 loops on hook) twice (Fdc made); rep from * for indicated number of foundation sts.

Front post double crochet (FPdc): Yo, insert hook from front to back and then to front again around post of indicated st, yo and draw up a loop, (yo and draw through 2 loops on hook) twice.

Front post treble crochet (FPtr): Yo twice, insert hook from front to back and then to front again around post of indicated st 2 rows below, yo and draw up a loop, [yo and draw through 2 loops on hook] 3 times.

1-over-1 front post double crochet left cross cable (1/1 FPdc LC) (worked over 2 sts): Sk next st, FPdc around next st 2 rows below; working in front of FPdc just made, FPdc around skipped st 2 rows below.

1-over-1 front post double crochet right cross cable (1/1 FPdc RC) (worked over 2 sts): Sk next st, FPdc around next st 2 rows below; working behind FPdc just made, FPdc around skipped st 2 rows below.

2-over-2 front post treble crochet left cross cable (2/2 FPtr LC) (worked over 4 sts): Sk next 2 sts, FPtr around each of next 2 sts 2 rows below; working in front of FPtr just made, FPtr around each of 2 skipped sts 2 rows below.

2-over-2 front post treble crochet right cross cable (2/2 FPtr RC) (worked over 4 sts): Sk next 2 sts, FPtr around each of next 2 sts 2 rows below; working behind FPtr just made, FPtr around each of 2 skipped sts 2 rows below.

Left leaning front post treble crochet (Left Leaning FPtr): FPtr around next st 2 rows below and 2 sts to the right of current st.

Right leaning front post treble crochet (Right Leaning FPtr): FPtr around next st 2 rows below and 2 sts to the left of current st.

3-double crochet fan (3-dc fan): 3 dc in indicated st or sp.

Front post double crochet V-stitch (FPdc-V): (FPdc, ch 1, FPdc) around post of indicated st.

First double crochet (First-dc): Sc in first st, ch 2. *Note:* Use this st whenever the first st of a row is a dc. When working back in the First-dc at the end of the following row, insert hook into the second ch of the ch-2.

Double crochet V-stitch (Dc-V): (Dc, ch 1, dc) in indicated st or sp.

PATTERN STITCHES

Raised front double crochet V-stitch and fans (Raised Front Dc-V and Fans) (worked on a multiple of 3 + 2 sts)

Swatch: 41 sts and 17 rows (+1 Fsc row)

Foundation Row: Work 41 Fsc, turn.

Row 1 (RS): First-dc, sk next st, Dc-V in next st, *sk next 2 sts, Dc-V in next st; rep from * to last 2 sts, sk next st, dc in last st, turn.

Row 2: First-dc, *3-dc fan in ch-1 sp of next Dc-V; rep from * to last st, dc in last st, turn.

Row 3: First-dc, sk next st, FPdc-V around next st, *sk next 2 sts, FPdc-V around next st; rep from * to last 2 sts, sk next st, dc in last st, turn.

Rep rows 2 and 3 for pattern st.

Sleeve Cable (worked on a multiple of 10 sts)

Row 1: Ch 1, sc in first st and in each st to end of row, turn.

Row 2 (RS): Work 1/1 FPdc LC, sc in next st, FPdc around each of next 4 sts 2 rows below, sc in next st, work 1/1 FPdc LC.

Row 3: Rep row 1.

Row 4: Work 1/1 FPdc LC, sc in next st, work 2/2 FPtr LC, sc in next st, work 1/1 FPdc LC.

Rep rows 1–4 for pattern st.

Raised Front Dc-V and Fans

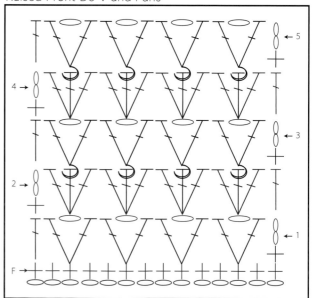

Trellis Cable (worked on a multiple of 44 sts)

Row 1: Ch 1, sc in first st and in each st to end of row, turn.

Row 2 (RS): Work 1/1 FPdc LC, sc in next st, FPdc around each of next 4 sts 2 rows below, sc in next st, work 1/1 FPdc LC, sc in each of next 10 sts, work 2/2 FPtr RC, sc in each of next 10 sts, work 1/1 FPdc RC, sc in next st, FPdc around each of next 4 sts 2 rows below, sc in next st, work 1/1 FPdc RC.

Row 3: Rep row 1.

Row 4: Work 1/1 FPdc LC, sc in next st, work 2/2 FPtr LC, sc in next st, work 1/1 FPdc LC, sc in each of next 8 sts, work Right Leaning FPtr twice, sc in each of next 4 sts, work Left Leaning FPtr twice, sc in each of next 8 sts, work 1/1 FPdc RC, sc in next st, work 2/2 FPtr RC, sc in next st, work 1/1 FPdc RC.

Row 5: Rep row 1.

Row 6: Work 1/1 FPdc LC, sc in next st, FPdc around each of next 4 sts 2 rows below, sc in next st, work 1/1 FPdc LC, sc in each of next 6 sts, work 2/2 FPtr RC, sc in each of next 4 sts, work 2/2 FPtr LC, sc in each of next 6 sts, work 1/1 FPdc RC, sc in next st, FPdc around each of next 4 sts 2 rows below, sc in next st, work 1/1 FPdc RC.

Row 7: Rep row 1.

Row 8: Work 1/1 FPdc LC, sc in next st, work 2/2 FPtr LC, sc in next st, work 1/1 FPdc LC, sc in each of next 4 sts, [work Right Leaning FPtr twice, sc in each of next 4 sts, work Left Leaning FPtr twice] twice, sc in each of next 4 sts, work 1/1 FPdc RC, sc in next st, work 2/2 FPtr RC, sc in next st, work 1/1 FPdc RC.

Row 9: Rep row 1.

Row 10: Work 1/1 FPdc LC, sc in next st, FPdc around each of next 4 sts 2 rows below, sc in next st, work 1/1 FPdc LC, sc in each of next 2 sts, work Right Leaning FPtr twice, sc in each of next 6 sts, work 2/2 FPtr LC, sc in each of next 6 sts, work Left Leaning FPtr twice, sc in each of next 2 sts, work 1/1 FPdc RC, sc in next st, FPdc around each of next 4 sts 2 rows below, sc in next st, work 1/1 FPdc RC.

Row 11: Rep row 1.

Row 12: Work 1/1 FPdc LC, sc in next st, work 2/2 FPtr LC, sc in next st, work 1/1 FPdc LC, sc in each of next 2 sts, FPdc around each of next 2 sts 2 rows below, sc in each of next 6 sts, FPdc around each of next 4 sts 2 rows below, sc in each of next 6 sts, FPdc around each of next 2 sts 2 rows below, sc in each of next 2 sts, work 1/1 FPdc RC, sc in next st, work 2/2 FPtr RC, sc in next st, work 1/1 FPdc RC.

Row 13: Rep row 1.

Row 14: Work 1/1 FPdc LC, sc in next st, [FPdc around next st 2 rows below] 4 times, sc in next st, work 1/1 FPdc LC, sc in each of next 4 sts, work Left Leaning FPtr twice, sc in each of next 4 sts, work 2/2 FPtr LC, sc in each of next 4 sts, work Right Leaning FPtr twice, sc in each of next 4 sts, work 1/1 FPdc RC, sc in next st, FPdc around each of next 4 sts 2 rows below, sc in next st, work 1/1 FPdc RC.

Row 15: Rep row 1.

Row 16: Work 1/1 FPdc LC, sc in next st, work 2/2 FPtr LC, sc in next st, work 1/1 FPdc LC, sc in each of next 6 sts, work Left Leaning FPtr twice, work Right Leaning FPtr twice, sc in each of next 4 sts, work Left Leaning FPtr twice, work Right Leaning FPtr twice, sc in each of next 6 sts, work 1/1 FPdc RC, sc in next st, work 2/2 FPtr RC, sc in next st, work 1/1 FPdc RC.

Row 17: Rep row 1.

Row 18: Work 1/1 FPdc LC, sc in next st, FPdc around each of next 4 sts 2 rows below, sc in next st, work 1/1 FPdc LC, sc in each of next 6 sts, work 2/2 FPtr LC, sc in each of next 4 sts, work 2/2 FPtr RC, sc in each of next 6 sts, work 1/1 FPdc RC, sc in next st, FPdc around each of next 4 sts 2 rows below, sc in next st, work 1/1 FPdc RC.

Row 19: Rep row 1.

Row 20: Work 1/1 FPdc LC, sc in next st, work 2/2 FPtr LC, sc in next st, work 1/1 FPdc LC, sc in each of next 4 sts, work 2/2 FPtr RC, sc in each of next 2 sts, work Left Leaning FPtr twice, work Right Leaning FPtr twice, sc in each of next 2 sts, work 2/2 FPtr LC, sc in each of next 4 sts, work 1/1 FPdc RC, sc in next st, work 2/2 FPtr RC, sc in next st, work 1/1 FPdc RC.

Row 21: Rep row 1.

Row 22: Work 1/1 FPdc LC, sc in next st, FPdc around each of next 4 sts 2 rows below, sc in next st, work 1/1 FPdc LC, sc in each of next 2 sts, work Right Leaning FPtr twice, sc in each of next 4 sts, work Left Leaning FPtr twice, work 2/2 FPtr RC, work Right Leaning FPtr twice, sc in each of next 4 sts, work Left Leaning FPtr twice, sc in each of next 2 sts, work 1/1 FPdc RC, sc in next st, FPdc around each of next 4 sts 2 rows below, sc in next st, work 1/1 FPdc RC.

Row 23: Rep row 1.

Row 24: Work 1/1 FPdc LC, sc in next st, work 2/2 FPtr LC, sc in next st, work 1/1 FPdc LC, sc in each of next 2 sts, FPdc around each of next 2 sts 2 rows below, sc in each of next 4 sts, work 2/2 FPtr LC twice, sc in each of next 4 sts, FPdc around each of next 2 sts 2 rows below, sc in each of next 2 sts, work 1/1 FPdc RC, sc in next st, work 2/2 FPtr RC, sc in next st, work 1/1 FPdc RC.

Row 25: Rep row 1.

Row 26: Work 1/1 FPdc LC, sc in next st, FPdc around each of next 4 sts 2 rows below, sc in next st, work 1/1 FPdc LC, sc in each of next 4 sts, work Left Leaning FPtr twice, work Right Leaning FPtr twice, sc in each of next 2 sts, work 2/2 FPtr RC, sc in each of next 2 sts, work Left Leaning FPtr twice, work Right Leaning FPtr twice, sc in each of next 4 sts, work 1/1 FPdc RC, sc in next st, FPdc around each of next 4 sts 2 rows below, sc in next st, work 1/1 FPdc RC.

Row 27: Rep row 1.

Trellis Cable

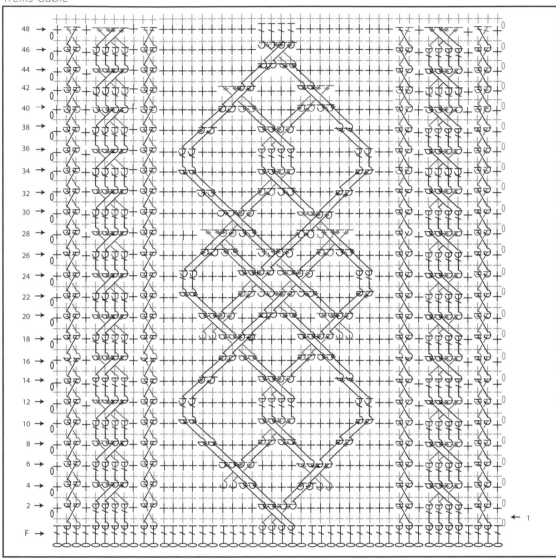

Row 28: Work 1/1 FPdc LC, sc in next st, work 2/2 FPtr LC, sc in next st, work 1/1 FPdc LC, sc in each of next 4 sts, work 2/2 FPtr LC, work Right Leaning FPtr twice, sc in each of next 4 sts, work Left Leaning FPtr twice, work 2/2 FPtr RC, sc in each of next 4 sts, work 1/1 FPdc RC, sc in next st, work 2/2 FPtr RC, sc in next st, work 1/1 FPdc RC.

Row 29: Rep row 1.

Rows 30–43: Rep rows 6–19.

Row 44: Work 1/1 FPdc LC, sc in next st, work 2/2 FPtr LC, sc in next st, work 1/1 FPdc LC, sc in each of next 10 sts, work Left Leaning FPtr twice, work Right Leaning FPtr twice, sc in each of next 10 sts, work 1/1 FPdc RC, sc in next st, work 2/2 FPtr RC, sc in next st, work 1/1 FPdc RC.

Row 45: Rep row 1.

Row 46: Work 1/1 FPdc LC, sc in next st, FPdc around each of next 4 sts 2 rows below, sc in next st, work 1/1 FPdc LC, sc in each of next 10 sts, work 2/2 FPtr RC, sc in each of next 10 sts, work 1/1 FPdc RC, sc in next st, FPdc around each of next 4 sts 2 rows below, sc in next st, work 1/1 FPdc RC.

Row 47: Rep row 1.

Row 48: Work 1/1 FPdc LC, sc in next st, work 2/2 FPtr LC, sc in next st, work 1/1 FPdc LC, sc in each of next 10 sts, FPdc around each of next 4 sts 2 rows below, sc in each of next 10 sts, work 1/1 FPdc RC, sc in next st, work 2/2 FPtr RC, sc in next st, work 1/1 FPdc RC.

Row 49: Rep row 1.

NOTE: To make a swatch for Trellis Cable pattern stitch, work as follows:

Swatch: 46 sts and 49 rows (+1 Fdc row)

Foundation Row: Work 46 Fdc, turn.

Work rows 1–49 of Trellis Cable pattern st adding "Ch 1, sc in first sc" at the beginning of each row and "sc in next st, turn." at the end of each row.

Block finished swatch to approximately 10 x 10.5".

SPECIAL TECHNIQUES

Knotless Starting Chain (see Special Techniques, p. 103)
End Cap Finishing Stitch (see Special Techniques, p. 108)
Locking Mattress Stitch (see Special Techniques, p. 104)

NOTES

1. When instructed to work in stitch 2 rows below, insert hook in indicated stitch in the row numbered 2 less than the row you are working. For example, if you are working row 5, a stitch "2 rows below" worked in row 3 (row 5 – 2 = row 3). When working "2 rows below," stitch of current row will remain unworked.

2. When instructed to increase 1 stitch at beginning and end of row, work as follows: Ch 1, sc in first st, sc 2 times in next st, [work in pattern as instructed to last 2 sts in row], sc 2 times in next st, sc in last st, turn. This will create one additional stitch at the beginning of the row and one additional stitch at the end of the row.

3. When instructed to work in a pattern "as established," work the next row of pattern and ensure that the stitches line up as in previous rows.

INSTRUCTIONS

Back Panel

Foundation Row: Work 82 (92, 102, 110, 120, 130, 138, 148) Fdc, turn.

Row 1: Ch 1, sc in first st and in each st to end of row, turn.

Row 2 (RS): Ch 1, sc in each of first 19 (24, 29, 33, 38, 43, 47, 52) sts, work 1/1 FPdc LC, sc in next st, FPdc around each of next 4 sts 2 rows below, sc in next st, work 1/1 FPdc LC, sc in each of next 24 sts, work 1/1 FPdc RC, sc in next 19 (24, 29, 33, 38, 43, 47, 52) sts, turn.

Row 3: Rep row 1.

Row 4: Ch 1, sc in each of first 19 (24, 29, 33, 38, 43, 47, 52) sts, work 1/1 FPdc LC, sc in next st, work 2/2 FPtr LC, sc in next st, work 1/1 FPdc LC, sc in each of next 24 sts, work 1/1 FPdc RC, sc in each of next 19 (24, 29, 33, 38, 43, 47, 52) sts, turn.

Row 5: Rep row 1.

Row 6: Ch 1, sc in each of first 19 (24, 29, 33, 38, 43, 47, 52) sts, work 1/1 FPdc LC, sc in next st, FPdc around each of next 4 sts 2 rows below, sc in next st, work 1/1 FPdc LC, sc in each of next 24 sts, work 1/1 FPdc RC, sc in next st, FPdc around each of next 4 sts 2 rows below, sc in next st, work 1/1 FPdc RC, sc in each of next 19 (24, 29, 33, 38, 43, 47, 52) sts, turn.

Row 7: Rep row 1.

Row 8: Ch 1, sc in each of first 19 (24, 29, 33, 38, 43, 47, 52) sts, work 1/1 FPdc LC, sc in next st, work 2/2 FPtr LC, sc in next st, work 1/1 FPdc LC, sc in each of next 24 sts, work 1/1 FPdc RC, sc in next st, work 2/2 FPtr RC, sc in next st, work 1/1 FPdc RC, sc in each of next 19 (24, 29, 33, 38, 43, 47, 52) sts, turn.

Row 9: Rep row 1.

Row 10: Ch 1, sc in each of first 19 (24, 29, 33, 38, 43, 47, 52) sts, work 1/1 FPdc LC, sc in next st, FPdc around each of next 4 sts 2 rows below, sc in next st, work 1/1 FPdc LC, sc in each of next 24 sts, work 1/1 FPdc RC, sc in next st, FPdc around each of next 4 sts 2 rows below, sc in next st, work 1/1 FPdc RC, sc in each of next 19 (24, 29, 33, 38, 43, 47, 52) sts, turn.

Row 11: Rep row 1.

Row 12: Ch 1, sc in each of first 19 (24, 29, 33, 38, 43, 47, 52) sts, work 1/1 FPdc LC, sc in next st, work 2/2 FPtr LC, sc in next st, work 1/1 FPdc LC, sc in each of next 24 sts, work 1/1 FPdc RC, sc in next st, work 2/2 FPtr RC, sc in next st, work 1/1 FPdc RC, sc in each of next 19 (24, 29, 33, 38, 43, 47, 52) sts, turn.

Sizes L (1X, 2X, 3X, 4X, 5X) Only

Row 13: Rep row 1.

Row 14: Ch 1, sc in each of first 29 (33, 38, 43, 47, 52) sts, work 1/1 FPdc LC, sc in next st, FPdc around each of next 4 sts 2 rows below, sc in next st, work 1/1 FPdc LC, sc in each of next 24 sts, work 1/1 FPdc RC, sc in next st, FPdc around each of next 4 sts 2 rows below, sc in next st, work 1/1 FPdc RC, sc in each of next 29 (33, 38, 43, 47, 52) sts, turn.

Row 15: Rep row 1.

Row 16: Ch 1, sc in each of first 29 (33, 38, 43, 47, 52) sts, work 1/1 FPdc LC, sc in next st, work 2/2 FPtr LC, sc in next st, work 1/1 FPdc LC, sc in each of next 24 sts, work 1/1 FPdc RC, sc in next st, work 2/2 FPtr RC, sc in next st, work 1/1 FPdc RC, sc in each of next 29 (33, 38, 43, 47, 52) sts, turn.

Sizes 2X (3X, 4X, 5X) Only

Row 17: Rep row 1.

Row 18: Ch 1, sc in each of first 38 (43, 47, 52) sts, work 1/1 FPdc LC, sc in next st, FPdc around each of next 4 sts 2 rows below, sc in next st, work 1/1 FPdc LC, sc in each of next 24 sts, work 1/1 FPdc RC, sc in next st, FPdc around each of next 4 sts 2 rows below, sc in next st, work 1/1 FPdc RC, sc in each of next 38 (43, 47, 52) sts, turn.

Row 19: Rep row 1.

Row 20: Ch 1, sc in each of first 38 (43, 47, 52) sts, work 1/1 FPdc LC, sc in next st, work 2/2 FPtr LC, sc in next st, work 1/1 FPdc LC, sc in each of next 24 sts, work 1/1 FPdc RC, sc in next st, work 2/2 FPtr RC, sc in next st, work 1/1 FPdc RC, sc in each of next 38 (43, 47, 52) sts, turn.

All Sizes

Begin Main Cable

Row 1: Work row 1 of Trellis Cable pattern st.

Row 2 (RS): Ch 1, sc in each of first 19 (24, 29, 33, 38, 43, 47, 52) sts, work row 2 of Trellis Cable pattern st, sc in each of next 19 (24, 29, 33, 38, 43, 47, 52) sts, turn.

Row 3: Work row 3 of Trellis Cable pattern st.

Row 4: Ch 1, sc in each of first 19 (24, 29, 33, 38, 43, 47, 52) sts, work row 4 of Trellis Cable pattern st, sc in each of next 19 (24, 29, 33, 38, 43, 47, 52) sts, turn.

Row 5: Work row 5 of Trellis Cable pattern st.

Row 6: Ch 1, sc in each of first 19 (24, 29, 33, 38, 43, 47, 52) sts, work row 6 of Trellis Cable pattern st, sc in each of next 19 (24, 29, 33, 38, 43, 47, 52) sts, turn.

Row 7: Work row 7 of Trellis Cable pattern st.

Row 8: Ch 1, sc in each of first 19 (24, 29, 33, 38, 43, 47, 52) sts, work row 8 of Trellis Cable pattern st, sc in each of next 19 (24, 29, 33, 38, 43, 47, 52) sts, turn.

Row 9: Work row 9 of Trellis Cable pattern st.

Row 10: Ch 1, sc in each of first 19 (24, 29, 33, 38, 43, 47, 52) sts, work row 10 of Trellis Cable pattern st, sc in each of next 19 (24, 29, 33, 38, 43, 47, 52) sts, turn.

Row 11: Work row 11 of Trellis Cable pattern st.

Row 12: Ch 1, sc in each of first 19 (24, 29, 33, 38, 43, 47, 52) sts, work row 12 of Trellis Cable pattern st, sc in each of next 19 (24, 29, 33, 38, 43, 47, 52) sts, turn.

Row 13: Work row 13 of Trellis Cable pattern st.

Row 14: Ch 1, sc in each of first 19 (24, 29, 33, 38, 43, 47, 52) sts, work row 14 of Trellis Cable pattern st, sc in each of next 19 (24, 29, 33, 38, 43, 47, 52) sts, turn.

Row 15: Work row 15 of Trellis Cable pattern st.

Row 16: Ch 1, sc in each of first 19 (24, 29, 33, 38, 43, 47, 52) sts, work row 16 of Trellis Cable pattern st, sc in each of next 19 (24, 29, 33, 38, 43, 47, 52) sts, turn.

Row 17: Work row 17 of Trellis Cable pattern st.

Row 18: Ch 1, sc in each of first 19 (24, 29, 33, 38, 43, 47, 52) sts, work row 18 of Trellis Cable pattern st, sc in each of next 19 (24, 29, 33, 38, 43, 47, 52) sts, turn.

Row 19: Work row 19 of Trellis Cable pattern st.

Row 20: Ch 1, sc in each of first 19 (24, 29, 33, 38, 43, 47, 52) sts, work row 20 of Trellis Cable pattern st, sc in each of next 19 (24, 29, 33, 38, 43, 47, 52) sts, turn.

Row 21: Work row 21 of Trellis Cable pattern st.

Row 22: Ch 1, sc in each of first 19 (24, 29, 33, 38, 43, 47, 52) sts, work row 22 of Trellis Cable pattern st, sc in each of next 19 (24, 29, 33, 38, 43, 47, 52) sts, turn.

Row 23: Work row 23 of Trellis Cable pattern st.

Row 24: Ch 1, sc in each of first 19 (24, 29, 33, 38, 43, 47, 52) sts, work row 24 of Trellis Cable pattern st, sc in each of next 19 (24, 29, 33, 38, 43, 47, 52) sts, turn.

Row 25: Work row 25 of Trellis Cable pattern st.

Row 26: Ch 1, sc in each of first 19 (24, 29, 33, 38, 43, 47, 52) sts, work row 26 of Trellis Cable pattern st, sc in each of next 19 (24, 29, 33, 38, 43, 47, 52) sts, turn.

Row 27: Work row 27 of Trellis Cable pattern st.

Row 28: Ch 1, sc in each of first 19 (24, 29, 33, 38, 43, 47, 52) sts, work row 28 of Trellis Cable pattern st, sc in each of next 19 (24, 29, 33, 38, 43, 47, 52) sts, turn.

Row 29: Work row 29 of Trellis Cable pattern st.

Rows 30–77: Rep rows 6–29, 2 more times.

Rows 78–91: Work rows 30–43 of Trellis Cable pattern st.

Row 92: Ch 1, sc in each of first 19 (24, 29, 33, 38, 43, 47, 52) sts, work row 44 of Trellis Cable pattern st, sc in each of next 19 (24, 29, 33, 38, 43, 47, 52) sts, turn.

Row 93: Work row 45 of Trellis Cable pattern st.

Row 94: Ch 1, sc in each of first 19 (24, 29, 33, 38, 43, 47, 52) sts, work row 46 of Trellis Cable pattern st, sc in each of next 19 (24, 29, 33, 38, 43, 47, 52) sts, turn.

Row 95: Work row 47 of Trellis Cable pattern st.

Row 96: Ch 1, sc in each of first 19 (24, 29, 33, 38, 43, 47, 52) sts, work row 48 of Trellis Cable pattern st, sc in each of next 19 (24, 29, 33, 38, 43, 47, 52) sts, turn.

Row 97: Work row 49 of Trellis Cable pattern st.

Row 98: Ch 1, sc in each of first 19 (24, 29, 33, 38, 43, 47, 52) sts, work 1/1 FPdc LC, sc in next st, FPdc around each of next 4 sts 2 rows below, sc in next st, work 1/1 FPdc LC, sc in each of next 24 sts, work 1/1 FPdc RC, sc in next st, FPdc around each of next 4 sts 2 rows below, sc in next st, work 1/1 FPdc RC, sc in each of next 19 (24, 29, 33, 38, 43, 47, 52) sts, turn.

Row 99: Rep row 1.

Row 100: Ch 1, sc in each of first 19 (24, 29, 33, 38, 43, 47, 52) sts, work 1/1 FPdc LC, sc in next st, work 2/2 FPtr LC, sc in next st, work 1/1 FPdc LC, sc in each of next 24 sts, work 1/1 FPdc RC, sc in next st, work 2/2 FPtr RC, sc in next st, work 1/1 FPdc RC, sc in each of next 19 (24, 29, 33, 38, 43, 47, 52) sts, turn.

Rows 101–107 (109, 107, 109, 107, 111, 113, 115): Rep last 4 rows.

Cut yarn, leaving tail for weaving in; pull tail through last st made; weave in tail using End Cap Finishing Stitch.

Front Panel (make 2)

Foundation Row: Work 89 (98, 107, 116, 125, 134, 146, 155) Fsc, turn.

Rows 1–57 (59, 59, 61, 61, 64, 65, 65): Work in Raised Front Dc-V and Fans pattern st.

Sizes S (L, 2X, 5X) Only

Row 58 (60, 62, 66): Rep row 2 once more.

All Sizes

Cut yarn, leaving tail for weaving in; pull tail through last st made; weave in tail using End Cap Finishing Stitch.

Sleeve (make 2)

Foundation Row: Work 46 (46, 46, 50, 50, 54, 56, 56) Fsc, turn.

Row 1: Ch 1, sc in first st and in each st to end of row, turn.

Row 2 (RS): Ch 1, sc in each of first 18 (18, 18, 20, 20, 22, 23, 23) sts, work row 1 of Sleeve Cable pattern st, sc in each of next 18 (18, 18, 20, 20, 22, 23, 23) sts, turn.

Row 3: Rep row 1.

Row 4: Ch 1, sc in each of first 18 (18, 18, 20, 20, 22, 23, 23) sts, work row 4 of Sleeve Cable pattern st, sc in each of next 18 (18, 18, 20, 20, 22, 23, 23) sts, turn.

Rows 5–84 (86, 88, 88, 93, 97, 99, 99): Continue to work in Sleeve Cable pattern st as established and increase as follows:

First, increase 1 st at beginning and end of every 7 (5, 5, 5, 5, 5, 5, 5) rows 6 (4, 16, 16, 13, 13, 11, 3) times—58 (54, 78, 82, 76, 80, 78, 62) sts.

Then, increase 1 st at beginning and end of every 6 (6, 4, 4, 4, 4, 4, 4) rows 7 (11, 2, 2, 7, 7, 11, 21) times—72 (76, 82, 86, 90, 94, 100, 104) sts.

Top of Sleeve Lace Border

With WS facing, join yarn in first st; first st of Transition Row is worked in same st as joining.

Sizes S (M, 2X, 3X, 4X, 5X) Only

Transition Row: Ch 1, [sc in each of first 23 (14, 14, 18, 19, 14) sts, sc 2 times in next st] 2 (4, 5, 4, 4, 6) times, sc in each of next 24 (16, 15, 18, 20, 14) sts, turn—74 (80, 95, 98, 104, 110) sts.

Sizes L (1X) Only

Transition Row: Ch 1, sc in each of first 17 (21) sts, [sc 2 times in next st, sc in each of next 15 (21) sts] 3 (2) times, sc 2 times in next st, sc in each of next 16 (20) sts, turn—86 (89) sts.

All Sizes

Rows 1–3: Work rows 1–3 of Raised Front Dc-V and Fans pattern st.

Row 4: Rep row 2.

Cut yarn, leaving tail for weaving in; pull tail through last st made; weave in tail using End Cap Finishing Stitch.

Cuff Lace Border

With WS facing, join yarn in first st; first st of Transition Row is worked in same st as joining.

Sizes S (M, L, 3X, 4X, 5X) Only

Transition Row: Ch 1, [sc in each for first 22 (22, 22, 17, 13, 13) sts, sc 2 times in next st] 1 (1, 1, 2, 3, 3) time(s), sc in each of next 23 (23, 23, 18, 14, 14) sts, turn—47 (47, 47, 56, 59, 59) sts.

Sizes 1X (2X) Only

Transition Row: Ch 1, sc in each of first 12 sts, [sc 2 times in next st, sc in each of next 12 sts] twice, sc 2 times in next st, sc in each of next 11 sts, turn—53 sts.

All Sizes

Rows 1–3: Work rows 1–3 of Raised Front Dc-V and Fans pattern st.

Row 4: Rep row 2.

Cut yarn, leaving tail for weaving in; pull tail through last st made; weave in tail using End Cap Finishing Stitch.

FINISHING

Block all pieces to measurements in schematic.
Using Locking Mattress Stitch, attach Front Panels to Back Panel by sewing 5.5 (6.5, 7, 8, 8.5, 9.3, 10, 11)"/13.5 (16.5, 18, 20.5, 21.5, 23.5, 25.5, 28) cm shoulder seams in preparation for making Top Lace Border.

Top Lace Border

With RS facing, join yarn in front corner of right Front Panel. First st of Row 1 is made in same st as joining.

Row 1: Work in Raised Front Dc-V and Fans pattern st as established across right Front Panel; work evenly in Raised Front Dc-V and Fans pattern st across back of neckline; reestablish and work Raised Front Dc-V and Fans pattern st as established across left Front Panel, turn.

Rows 2–4: Work in Raised Front Dc-V and Fans pattern st as established.

Cut yarn, leaving tail for weaving in; pull tail through last st made; weave in tail using End Cap Finishing Stitch.
Block Top Lace Border to match Front Panels.
Fold Sleeves in half lengthwise. Matching fold to shoulder seam, sew top of Sleeves to Front and Back. Sew top of sleeve and underarm seams. Sew side body seams.
Weave in all ends.

Five Easy Pieces Schematic

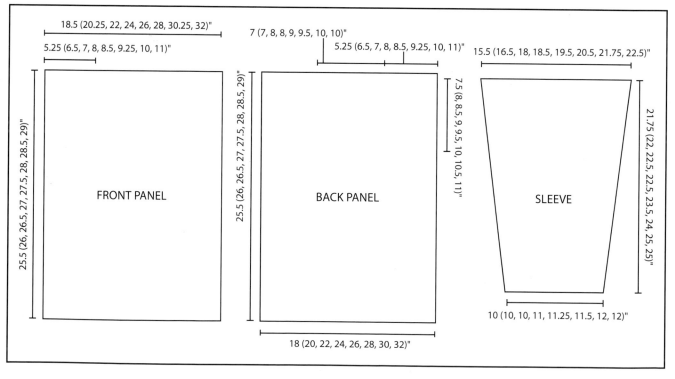

18.5 (20.25, 22, 24, 26, 28, 30.25, 32)"

5.25 (6.5, 7, 8, 8.5, 9.25, 10, 11)"

7 (7, 8, 8, 9, 9.5, 10, 10)"

5.25 (6.5, 7, 8, 8.5, 9.25, 10, 11)"

15.5 (16.5, 18, 18.5, 19.5, 20.5, 21.75, 22.5)"

25.5 (26, 26.5, 27, 27.5, 28, 28.5, 29)"

7.5 (8, 8.5, 9, 9.5, 10, 10.5, 11)"

21.75 (22, 22.5, 22.5, 23.5, 24, 25, 25)"

FRONT PANEL

BACK PANEL

SLEEVE

18 (20, 22, 24, 26, 28, 30, 32)"

10 (10, 10, 11, 11.25, 11.5, 12, 12)"

SHAWL COLLAR CARDIGAN

Rectangles and trapezoids are the ruling geometric figures in this design. Again, the simplicity of the shapes allowed us to take the luxurious texture stitches to a level that borders on decadence. You'll love how this fabric feels as you watch the pattern stitch dissipate up the body panels. And we all know nothing beats the feel of a luxurious ribbed shawl collar. This one is a wardrobe essential—ya gotta have one!

SKILL LEVEL: ⬛⬛⬜⬜
Easy

SIZES: S (M, L, XL, 2X, 3X, 4X, 5X)
Sample shown in size small

FINISHED MEASUREMENTS
To Fit Bust: 32 (36, 40, 44, 48, 52, 56, 60)"/81.5 (91.5, 101.5, 112, 122, 132, 142, 152.5) cm
Finished Bust: 35.5 (40.5, 44.25, 49, 52.75, 57.5, 61.25, 65)"/90 (103, 112.5, 124.5, 134, 146, 155.5, 165) cm
Finished Length from Shoulder: 28 (28, 28, 29, 29, 29, 30, 30)"/71 (71, 71, 73.5, 73.5, 73.5, 76, 76) cm

MATERIALS AND TOOLS

Sample uses Cascade, Heritage 150 (75% superwash merino wool, 25% nylon; 5.3 ounces/150 g per skein = 492 yds/450 m): 7 (8, 9, 10, 11, 11, 12, 13) hanks in color Radiant Orchid #5695—3444 (3936, 4428, 4920, 5412, 5412, 5904, 6396) yards/ 3150 (3600, 4049, 4499, 4949, 4949, 5399, 5849) m of fine-weight yarn
Crochet hooks: 3.25 mm (size D-3) and 3.50 mm (size E-4) or sizes to obtain gauge.
Yarn needle

BLOCKED GAUGES
Front post cluster texture stitch: 6.56 sts = 1"/2.5 cm; 41 sts = 6.25"/16 cm; 5.6 rows = 1"/2.5 cm; 35 rows = 6.25"/ 16 cm with larger hook
Single crochet ribbing: 6.36 sts = 1"/2.5 cm; 35 sts = 5.5"/14 cm; 6.74 rows = 1"/2.5 cm; 32 rows = 4.75"/12 cm with smaller hook

STITCH GUIDE

Foundation single crochet (Fsc): Ch 2, insert hook in 2nd ch from hook, yo and draw up a loop, yo and draw through 1 loop (first "chain" made), yo and draw through 2 loops on hook (first Fsc made), *insert hook under 2 loops of the "chain" just made, yo and draw up a loop, yo and draw through 1 loop ("chain" made), yo and draw through 2 loops on hook (Fsc made); rep from * for indicated number of foundation sts.

Front post cluster stitch (FP-Cl): Yo, insert hook from front to back to front again around post of indicated st, yo and draw up a loop, yo and draw through 2 loops on hook (2 loops remain on hook); yo, insert hook from front to back to front again around post of same st, yo and draw up a loop, yo and draw through 2 loops on hook; yo and draw through all 3 loops on hook.

Single crochet through back loop only (sc-tbl): Insert hook in back loop of indicated st, yo and draw up a loop, yo and draw through 2 loops on hook.

PATTERN STITCHES

Front post cluster texture stitch (FP-Cl Texture St) (worked on a multiple of 4 + 1 sts)

Swatch: 41 sts and 35 rows (+1 Fsc row)

Foundation Row: With larger hook, work 41 Fsc, turn.

Row 1 (RS): Ch 1, sc in first st, *ch 1, sk next st, sc in next st; rep from * across, turn.

Row 2: Ch 1, sc in first st, *ch 1, sk next ch-1 sp, sc in next st; rep from * across, turn.

Row 3: Ch 1, sc in first st, ch 1, sk next ch-1 sp, sc in next st, *ch 1, sk next ch-1 sp, FP-Cl around next st 2 rows below, ch 1, sk next ch-1 sp, sc in next st; rep from * to last ch-1 sp, ch 1, sk next ch-1 sp, sc in last st, turn.

Row 4: Rep row 2.

Row 5: Ch 1, sc in first st, *ch 1, sk next ch-1 sp, FP-Cl around next st 2 rows below, ch 1, sk next ch-1 sp, sc in next st; rep from * across, turn.

Rep rows 2–5 for pattern st.

Single crochet ribbing (sc ribbing) (worked on any number of sts)

Swatch: 35 sts and 31 rows (+1 Fsc row)

Foundation Row: With smaller hook, work 35 Fsc, turn.

Row 1: Ch 1, sc in both loops of first st, sc-tbl in each st across to last st, sc in both loops of last st, turn.

Rep row 1 for pattern st.

SPECIAL TECHNIQUES

Knotless Starting Chain (see Special Techniques, p. 103)
End Cap Finishing Stitch (see Special Techniques, p. 108)
Locking Mattress Stitch (see Special Techniques, p. 104)

NOTES

1. When instructed to work in stitch 2 rows below, insert hook in indicated stitch in the row numbered 2 less than the row you are working. For example, if you are working row 5, a stitch "2 rows below" is worked in row 3 (row 5 – 2 = row 3). When working "2 rows below," stitch of current row will remain unworked.

2. When instructed to increase 1 stitch at beginning and end of row, work as follows: Ch 1, sc in first st, sc 2 times in next st, [work in pattern as instructed to last 2 sts in row], sc 2 times in next st, sc in last st, turn. This will create one additional stitch at the beginning of the row and one additional stitch at the end of the row.

3. When instructed to work in a pattern "as established," work the next row of pattern and ensure that the stitches line up as in previous rows.

4. When instructed to work in pattern as established and increase in pattern when working sleeves, reestablish pattern as you add enough stitches to the beginning and end of the row to work another repeat of the pattern.

FP-Cl Texture Stitch

Sc ribbing

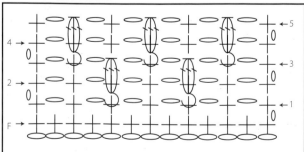

INSTRUCTIONS

Back

Foundation Row: With larger hook, work 117 (133, 145, 161, 173, 189, 201, 213) Fsc, turn.

Row 1 (RS): Ch 1, sc in first st, *ch 1, sk next st, sc in next st; rep from * to end of row, turn.

Rows 2–5: Rep rows 2–5 of FP-Cl Texture St.

Rows 6–33: Rep rows 2–5.

Rows 34–36: Rep rows 2–4.

Sizes S (M, 2X, 3X, 5X) Only

Row 37: Ch 1, sc in first st, *ch 1, sk next ch-1 sp, FP-Cl around next st 2 rows below, [ch 1, sk next ch-1 sp, sc in next st] 3 times; rep from * to last 4 sts, ch 1, sk next ch-1 sp, FP-Cl around next st 2 rows below, ch 1, sk next ch-1 sp, sc in last st, turn.

Row 38: Rep row 2.

Row 39: Ch 1, sc in first st, [ch 1, sk next ch-1 sp, sc in next st] twice, *ch 1, sk next ch-1 sp, FP-Cl around next st 2 rows below, [ch 1, sk next ch-1 sp, sc in next st] 3 times; rep from * to end of row, turn.

Row 40: Rep row 2.

Rows 41–44: Rep rows 37–40.

Sizes L (1X, 4X) Only

Row 37: Ch 1, sc in first st, *ch 1, sk next ch-1 sp, FP-Cl around next st 2 rows below, [ch 1, sk next ch-1 sp, sc in next st] 3 times; rep from * to end of row, turn.

Row 38: Rep row 2.

Row 39: Ch 1, sc in first st, [ch 1, sk next ch-1 sp, sc in next st] twice, *ch 1, sk next ch-1 sp, FP-Cl around next st 2 rows below, [ch 1, sk next ch-1 sp, sc in next st] 3 times; rep from * to last 4 sts, ch 1, sk next ch-1 sp, FP-Cl around next st 2 rows below, ch 1, sk next ch-1 sp, sc in last st, turn.

Row 40: Rep row 2.

Rows 41–44: Rep rows 37–40.

Sizes S (M, 5X) Only

Row 45: Ch 1, sc in first st, *ch 1, sk next ch-1 sp, FP-Cl around next st 2 rows below, [ch 1, sk next ch-1 sp] 7 times; rep from * to last 4 sts, ch 1, sk next ch-1 sp, FP-Cl around next st 2 rows below, ch 1, sk next ch-1 sp, sc in last st, turn.

Row 46: Rep row 2.

Row 47: Ch 1, sc in first st, [ch 1, sk next ch-2 sp, sc in next st] 4 times, *ch 1, sk next ch-1 sp, FP-Cl around next st 2 rows below, [ch 1, sk next ch-1 sp, sc in next st] 7 times; rep from * to last 12 sts, ch 1, sk next ch-1 sp, FP-Cl around next st 2 rows below, [ch 1, sk next ch-1 sp, sc in next st] 5 times, turn.

Sizes L (1X) Only

Row 45: Ch 1, sc in first st, *ch 1, sk next ch-1 sp, FP-Cl around next st 2 rows below, [ch 1, sk next ch-1 sp] 7 times; rep from * to end of row, turn.

Row 46: Rep row 2.

Row 47: Ch 1, sc in first st, [ch 1, sk next ch-2 sp, sc in next st] 4 times, *ch 1, sk next ch-1 sp, FP-Cl around next st 2 rows below, [ch 1, sk next ch-1 sp, sc in next st] 7 times; rep from * to last 8 sts, ch 1, sk next ch-1 sp, FP-Cl around next st 2 rows below, [ch 1, sk next ch-1 sp, sc in next st] 3 times, turn.

Sizes 2X (3X) Only

Row 45: Ch 1, sc in first st, *ch 1, sk next ch-1 sp, FP-Cl around next st 2 rows below, [ch 1, sk next ch-1 sp] 7 times; rep from * to last 12 sts, ch 1, sk next ch-1 sp, FP-Cl around next st 2 rows below, [ch 1, sk next ch-1 sp, sc in next st] 5 times, turn.

Row 46: Rep row 2.

Row 47: Ch 1, sc in first st, [ch 1, sk next ch-2 sp, sc in next st] 4 times, *ch 1, sk next ch-1 sp, FP-Cl around next st 2 rows below, [ch 1, sk next ch-1 sp, sc in next st] 7 times; rep from * to last 4 sts, ch 1, sk next ch-1 sp, FP-Cl around next st 2 rows below, ch 1, sk next ch-1 sp, sc in last st, turn.

Size 4X Only

Row 45: Ch 1, sc in first st, *ch 1, sk next ch-1 sp, FP-Cl around next st 2 rows below, [ch 1, sk next ch-1 sp] 7 times; rep from * to last 8 sts, ch 1, sk next ch-1 sp, FP-Cl around next st 2 rows below, [ch 1, sk next ch-1 sp, sc in next st] 3 times, turn.

Row 46: Rep row 2.

Row 47: Ch 1, sc in first st, [ch 1, sk next ch-2 sp, sc in next st] 4 times, *ch 1, sk next ch-1 sp, FP-Cl around next st 2 rows below, [ch 1, sk next ch-1 sp, sc in next st] 7 times; rep from * to end of row, turn.

All Sizes

Rows 48–50: Rep row 2.

Row 51: Rep row 45.

Rows 52–54: Rep row 2.

Row 55: Rep row 47.

Rows 56–60: Rep row 2.

Row 61: Rep row 45.

Rows 62–66: Rep row 2.

Row 67: Rep row 47.

Rows 68–74: Rep row 2.

Row 75: Rep row 45.

Rows 76–82: Rep row 2.

Row 83: Rep row 47.

Rows 84–99: Rep rows 68–83.

Rows 100–157 (157, 157, 162, 162, 162, 168, 168): Rep rows 68–83.

Cut yarn, leaving tail for weaving in; pull tail through last st made; weave in tail using End Cap Finishing Stitch.

Front (make 2)

Foundation Row: With larger hook, work 41 (45, 49, 53, 57, 57, 61, 69) Fsc, turn.

Row 1 (RS): Ch 1, sc in first st, *ch 1, sk next st, sc in next st; rep from * to end of row, turn.

Rows 2–5: Rep rows 2–5 of FP-Cl Texture St.

Rows 6–33: Rep rows 2–5.

Rows 34–36: Rep rows 2–4.

Sizes M (1X, 4X, 5X) Only

Row 37: Ch 1, sc in first st, *ch 1, sk next ch-1 sp, FP-Cl around next st 2 rows below, [ch 1, sk next ch-1 sp, sc in next st] 3 times; rep from * to last 4 sts, ch 1, sk next ch-1 sp, FP-Cl around next st 2 rows below, ch 1, sk next ch-1 sp, sc in last st, turn.

Row 38: Rep row 2.

Row 39: Ch 1, sc in first st, [ch 1, sk next ch-1 sp, sc in next st] twice, *ch 1, sk next ch-1 sp, FP-Cl around next st 2 rows below, [ch 1, sk next ch-1 sp, sc in next st] 3 times; rep from * to end of row, turn.

Row 40: Rep row 2.

Rows 41–44: Rep rows 37–40.

Sizes S (L, 2X, 3X) Only

Row 37: Ch 1, sc in first st, *ch 1, sk next ch-1 sp, FP-Cl around next st 2 rows below, [ch 1, sk next ch-1 sp, sc in next st] 3 times; rep from * to end of row, turn.

Row 38: Rep row 2.

Row 39: Ch 1, sc in first st, [ch 1, sk next ch-1 sp, sc in next st] twice, *ch 1, sk next ch-1 sp, FP-Cl around next st 2 rows below, [ch 1, sk next ch-1 sp, sc in next st] 3 times; rep from * to last 4 sts, ch 1, sk next ch-1 sp, FP-Cl around next st 2 rows below, ch 1, sk next ch-1 sp, sc in last st, turn.

Row 40: Rep row 2.

Rows 41–44: Rep rows 37–40.

Sizes S (2X, 3X) Only

Row 45: Ch 1, sc in first st, *ch 1, sk next ch-1 sp, FP-Cl around next st 2 rows below, [ch 1, sk next ch-1 sp] 7 times; rep from * to last 8 sts, ch 1, sk next ch-1 sp, FP-Cl around next st 2 rows below, [ch 1, sk next ch-1 sp, sc in next st] 3 times, turn.

Row 46: Rep row 2.

Row 47: Ch 1, sc in first st, [ch 1, sk next ch-2 sp, sc in next st] 4 times, *ch 1, sk next ch-1 sp, FP-Cl around next st 2 rows below, [ch 1, sk next ch-1 sp, sc in next st] 7 times; rep from * to end of row, turn.

Sizes M (4X) Only

Row 45: Ch 1, sc in first st, *ch 1, sk next ch-1 sp, FP-Cl around next st 2 rows below, [ch 1, sk next ch-1 sp] 7 times; rep from * to last 12 sts, ch 1, sk next ch-1 sp, FP-Cl around next st 2 rows below, [ch 1, sk next ch-1 sp, sc in next st] 5 times, turn.

Row 46: Rep row 2.

Row 47: Ch 1, sc in first st, [ch 1, sk next ch-2 sp, sc in next st] 4 times, *ch 1, sk next ch-1 sp, FP-Cl around next st 2 rows below, [ch 1, sk next ch-1 sp, sc in next st] 7 times; rep from * to last 4 sts, ch 1, sk next ch-1 sp, FP-Cl around next st 2 rows below, ch 1, sk next ch-1 sp, sc in last st, turn.

Sizes 1X (5X) Only

Row 45: Ch 1, sc in first st, *ch 1, sk next ch-1 sp, FP-Cl around next st 2 rows below, [ch 1, sk next ch-1 sp] 7 times; rep from * to last 4 sts, ch 1, sk next ch-1 sp, FP-Cl around next st 2 rows below, ch 1, sk next ch-1 sp, sc in last st, turn.

Row 46: Rep row 2.

Row 47: Ch 1, sc in first st, [ch 1, sk next ch-2 sp, sc in next st] 4 times, *ch 1, sk next ch-1 sp, FP-Cl around next st 2 rows below, [ch 1, sk next ch-1 sp, sc in next st] 7 times; rep from * to last 12 sts, ch 1, sk next ch-1 sp, FP-Cl around next st 2 rows below, [ch 1, sk next ch-1 sp, sc in next st] 5 times, turn.

Size L Only

Row 45: Ch 1, sc in first st, *ch 1, sk next ch-1 sp, FP-Cl around next st 2 rows below, [ch 1, sk next ch-1 sp] 7 times; rep from * to end of row, turn.

Row 46: Rep row 2.

Row 47: Ch 1, sc in first st, [ch 1, sk next ch-2 sp, sc in next st] 4 times, *ch 1, sk next ch-1 sp, FP-Cl around next st 2 rows below, [ch 1, sk next ch-1 sp, sc in next st] 7 times; rep from * to last 8 sts, ch 1, sk next ch-1 sp, FP-Cl around next st 2 rows below, [ch 1, sk next ch-1 sp, sc in next st] 3 times, turn.

All Sizes

Rows 48–50: Rep row 2.

Row 51: Rep row 45.

Rows 52–54: Rep row 2.

Row 55: Rep row 47.

Rows 56–60: Rep row 2.

Row 61: Rep row 45.

Rows 62–66: Rep row 2.

Row 67: Rep row 47.

Rows 68–74: Rep row 2.

Row 75: Rep row 45.

Rows 76–82: Rep row 2.

Row 83: Rep row 47.

Rows 84–99: Rep rows 68–83.

Rows 100–157 (157, 157, 162, 162, 162, 168, 168): Rep rows 68–83.

Cut yarn, leaving tail for weaving in; pull tail through last st made; weave in tail using End Cap Finishing Stitch.

Sleeve (make 2)

Foundation Row: With larger hook, work 61 (65, 69, 69, 73, 73, 77, 77) Fsc, turn.

Row 1 (RS): Ch 1, sc in first st, *ch 1, sk next st, sc in next st; rep from * to end of row, turn.

Rows 2–5: Rep rows 2–5 of FP-Cl Texture St.

Row 6: Rep row 2.

Rows 7–115 (115, 118, 118, 123, 126, 132, 132): Continue to work in FP-Cl Texture St as established and increasing in pattern as follows:

First, increase 1 st at beginning and end of every 6 (6, 5, 4, 4, 3, 3, 3) rows 10 (17, 14, 13, 18, 4, 2, 18) times—81 (99, 97, 95, 109, 81, 81, 113) sts.

Then, increase 1 st at beginning and end of every 7 (7, 6, 5, 5, 4, 4, 4) rows 7 (1, 7, 12, 9, 27, 30, 18) times—95 (101, 111, 119, 127, 135, 141, 149) sts.

Rows 116 (116, 119, 119, 124, 127, 133, 133)–126 (126, 129, 129, 134, 137, 143, 143): Work in FP-Cl Texture St as established without increasing.

Cut yarn, leaving tail for weaving in; pull tail through last st made; weave in tail using End Cap Finishing Stitch.

Collar

Foundation Row: With smaller hook, work 58 (58, 61, 61, 61, 64, 64, 64) Fsc, turn.

Rows 1–418 (422, 428, 444, 451, 454, 475, 475): Work in sc ribbing pattern st.

Cut yarn, leaving tail for weaving in; pull tail through last st made; weave in tail using End Cap Finishing Stitch.

FINISHING

Block all pieces to measurements in schematic.
Using Locking Mattress Stitch, sew seams as follows:
Sew Fronts to Back along shoulder seams, leaving approximately 6 (6.5, 7.5, 8, 9, 9.5, 10.5, 10.5)"/15 (16.5, 19, 20.5, 23, 24, 26.5, 26.5) cm for back neckline.
Sew side seams, leaving 7 (7.5, 8, 8.5, 9, 9.5, 10, 10.5)"/18 (19, 20.5, 21.5, 23, 24, 25.5, 26.5) cm opening for armholes.
Set Sleeves into armholes and sew into place.
Sew seam under Sleeves.
Pin center point of one long edge of Collar to center of back neckline; pin corners of same long edge of Collar to bottom front corners of garment; place pins to evenly distribute Collar rows around front garment border; sew Collar into place.
Weave in all ends.

Shawl Collar Cardi Schematic

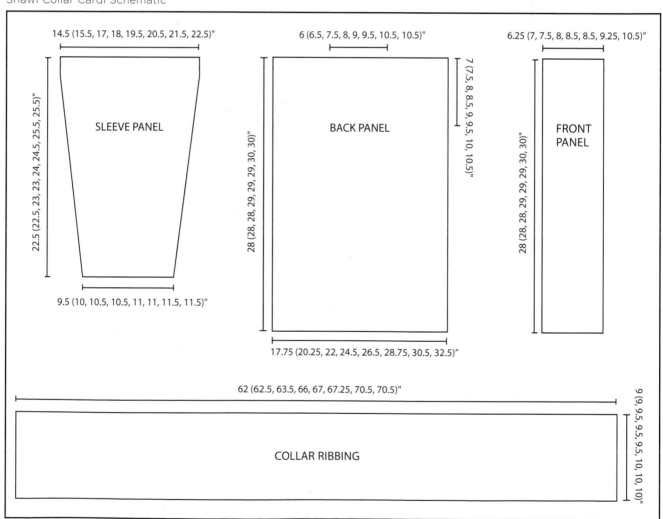

HALF CIRCLE CARDIGAN

Combining the best of circles, rectangles, and even triangular segments, this cardi is a showstopper. Intriguing textures grow into dramatic radiating lines that will captivate you as you make this piece and mesmerize those who see you wear it. A garment or a work of art? Both! You'll love watching this piece grow as the stitches roll off your hook, and you'll love the drape and feel of this one-of-a-kind cardi. Wear this piece right-side up, upside down, or even inside out . . . the stunning graphics and ultimate versatility of this piece will make it a favorite in your wardrobe.

SKILL LEVEL: ◖◻◼◼◻◗
Intermediate

SIZES: S (M, L, XL, 2X, 3X, 4X, 5X)
Sample shown in size small

FINISHED MEASUREMENTS
To Fit Bust: 32 (36, 40, 44, 48, 52, 56, 60)"/81.5 (91.5, 101.5, 112, 122, 132, 142, 152.5) cm
Finished Bust: 36 (40, 44, 48, 52, 56, 60, 64)"/91.5 (101.5, 112, 122, 132, 142, 152.5, 162.5) cm
Center Back Length from Shoulder: 28 (31, 32, 34.5, 36.25, 37.25, 39.5, 41.25)"/71 (78.5, 81.5, 87.5, 92, 94.5, 100.5, 105) cm

MATERIALS AND TOOLS

Sample uses Tahki, Cotton Classic Lite (100% mercerized cotton; 1.75 ounces/50 g = 146 yards/135 m): 8 (9, 10, 11, 12, 13, 14, 15) skeins in color Dark Bright Blue #4870—1168 (1314, 1460, 1606, 1752, 1898, 2044, 2190) yards/1069 (1202, 1336, 1469, 1603, 1736, 1870, 2003) m of lightweight yarn
Crochet hook: 3.50 mm (size E-4) or size to obtain gauge
Yarn needle
Stitch markers
Sample on p. 42 shown using 1, 1.5" Flame Pedestal Button by JUL Designs

BLOCKED GAUGE
Urban Grids: 5.54 sts = 1"/2.5 cm; 72 sts = 13"/33 cm; 3.29 rows = 1"/2.5 cm; 28 rows = 8.5"/21.5 cm

Top Border

Turn work one-quarter turn to the right so top edge is up and sides of end of row sts are ready for working into. Top Border sts are worked into sides of end of row sts.

Row 1: Ch 1, First-dc in side of last sc made, *work 3 dc into the side of next dc, dc in side of next sc; rep from * to end of row, turn—approximately** 132 (148, 152, 164, 172, 176, 188, 196) sts.

NOTE: If row 1 looks like it is starting to ripple, wave, ruffle, or otherwise go wonky, work fewer sts in side of each dc.

Row 2: First-dc, dc in each st to end of row, turn.

Cut yarn, leaving tail for weaving in; pull tail through last st made; weave in tail using End Cap Finishing Stitch.

FINISHING

Block to measurements in schematic.

Sleeves (make 2)

With RS of garment facing, join yarn in bottom of armhole opening. First st of rnd 1 is made in same st as joining.

Rnd 1: Ch 1, sc in each armhole border st around both sides of armhole opening. Be careful to join top and bottom of armhole securely with tight stitch, join rnd with sl st in first sc made, turn.

Rnd 2: First-dc, dc in next st and in each st to end of rnd, join rnd with sl st in First-dc, turn.

Rnd 3: Ch 1, BPsc around first st and around each st to end of rnd, join rnd with sl st in first BPsc made, turn.

Rnds 4–5: Rep rnds 2 and 3. Do not join last rnd with sl st.

Cut yarn, leaving tail for weaving in; pull tail through last st made; weave in tail using Duplicate Stitch.

Block sleeves to fit if needed.

Weave in all ends.

Half Circle Cardi Schematic

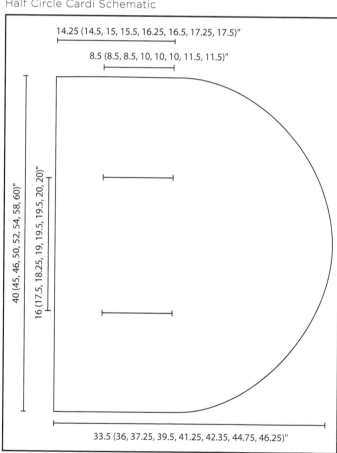

14.25 (14.5, 15, 15.5, 16.25, 16.5, 17.25, 17.5)"

8.5 (8.5, 8.5, 10, 10, 10, 11.5, 11.5)"

40 (45, 46, 50, 52, 54, 58, 60)"

16 (17.5, 18.25, 19, 19.5, 19.5, 20, 20)"

33.5 (36, 37.25, 39.5, 41.25, 42.35, 44.75, 46.25)"

PULLOVERS

T-TOP

We've given the functional and conventional T-top an upgrade to the extraordinary! Made from cuff to cuff, this silhouette is flattering on every body type and features a spectacular lace fabric based on our wildly popular woven cables pattern stitch. This is your new go-to piece when you want something that looks FAB while showing off your crochet proficiency.

SKILL LEVEL: ◼◼◼▭
Experienced

SIZES: S (M, L, XL, 2X, 3X, 4X, 5X)
Samples shown in size small and 3X

FINISHED MEASUREMENTS
To Fit Bust: 32 (36, 40, 44, 48, 52, 56, 60)"/81.5 (91.5, 101.5, 112, 122, 132, 142, 152.5) cm
Finished Bust: 36 (40, 44, 48, 52, 56, 60, 64)"/91.5 (101.5, 112, 122, 132, 142, 152.5, 162.5) cm
Finished Length from Shoulder: 27.25 (27.25, 28.5, 28.5, 29.75, 29.75, 29.75, 29.75)"/69 (69, 72.5, 72.5, 75.5, 75.5, 75.5, 75.5) cm

MATERIALS AND TOOLS

Sample uses Malabrigo, Sock (100% superwash merino wool; 3.5 ounces/100 g = 440 yards/402 m): 5 (6, 7, 7, 8, 8, 9, 10) balls; sample size small shown in color Lettuce #37-2200; sample size 3X shown in color Terracotta #SW802—2200 (2640, 3080, 3080, 3520, 3520, 3960, 4400) yards/2012 (2415, 2817, 2817, 3219, 3219, 3622, 4024) m of superfine-weight yarn
Crochet hook: 3.25 mm (size D-3) or size to obtain gauge
Yarn needle

BLOCKED GAUGE
Woven Cables Lace: 6.25 sts = 1"/2.5 cm; 50 sts = 8"/20.5 cm; 3 rows = 1"/2.5 cm; 18 rows = 6"/15 cm

STITCH GUIDE

Foundation single crochet (Fsc): Ch 2, insert hook in 2nd ch from hook, yo and draw up a loop, yo and draw through 1 loop (first "chain" made), yo and draw through 2 loops on hook (first Fsc made), *insert hook under 2 loops of the "chain" just made, yo and draw up a loop, yo and draw through 1 loop ("chain" made), yo and draw through 2 loops on hook (Fsc made); rep from * for indicated number of foundation sts.

Extending foundation single crochet (foundation sc as used for extending rows) (Ext-Fsc): Insert hook in last st worked, yo and draw up a loop, yo and draw through 1 loop (first "chain" made), yo and draw through 2 loops on hook (first Ext-Fsc made), *insert hook under 2 loops of the "chain" just made, yo and draw up a loop, yo and draw through 1 loop ("chain" made), yo and draw through 2 loops on hook (Ext-Fsc made); rep from * for desired number of extending foundation sts.

First treble crochet (First-tr): Sc in first st, ch 3. *Note:* Use this st whenever the first st of a row is a tr. When working back in the First-tr at the end of the following row, insert hook into the third ch of the ch-3.

Treble crochet (tr): Yo twice, insert hook into indicated st, yo and draw up a loop, (yo and draw through 2 loops on hook) 3 times.

Double treble crochet (dtr): Yo 3 times, insert hook into indicated st, yo and draw up a loop, (yo and draw through 2 loops on hook) 4 times.

Triple treble crochet (trtr): Yo 4 times, insert hook into indicated st, yo and draw up a loop, (yo and draw through 2 loops on hook) 5 times.

Front post treble crochet (FPtr): Yo twice, insert hook from front to back and then to front again around post of indicated st 2 rows below, yo and draw up a loop, [yo and draw through 2 loops on hook] 3 times.

Front post double treble crochet (FPdtr): Yo 3 times, insert hook from front to back and then to front again around post of indicated st, yo and draw up a loop, [yo and draw through 2 loops on hook] 4 times.

Front post triple treble crochet (FPtrtr): Yo 4 times, insert hook from front to back and then to front again around post of indicated st, yo and draw up a loop, [yo and draw through 2 loops on hook] 5 times.

3-over-3 double treble crochet left cross cable (3/3 dtr LC) (worked over 6 sts): Sk next 3 sts, dtr around each of next 3 sts, working in front of dtr just made, dtr in each of first 3 skipped sts.

3-over-3 front post double treble left cross cable (3/3 FPdtr LC) (worked over 6 sts): Sk next 3 sts, FPdtr around each of next 3 sts 2 rows below, working in front of FPdtr just made, FPdtr around each of first 3 skipped sts 2 rows below.

3-2-3 front post triple treble right cross cable (3-2-3 FPtrtr RC) (worked over 8 sts): Sk next 5 sts, FPtrtr around each of next 3 sts 2 rows below, ch 2, working behind FPtrtr and ch 2 just made, FPtrtr around each of first 3 skipped sts 2 rows below.

Woven Cables Lace

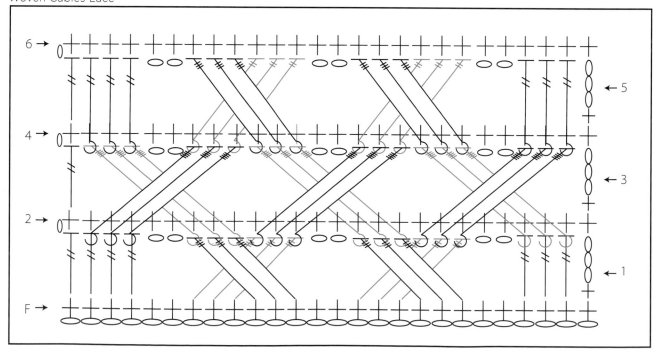

PATTERN STITCH

Woven Cables Lace (worked on a multiple of 8 + 2 sts)

Swatch: 50 sts and 18 rows (+1 Fsc row)

Foundation Row: Work 50 Fsc, turn.

Row 1 (RS): First-tr, tr around each of next 3 sts, ch 2, sk next 2 sts, *3/3 dtr LC, ch 2, sk next 2 sts; rep from * to last 4 sts, tr in each of last 4 sts, turn.

Row 2: Ch 1, sc in first st and in each st and ch to end of row, turn.

Row 3: First-tr, *3-2-3 FPtrtr RC; rep from * to last st, tr in last st, turn.

Row 4: Rep row 2.

Row 5: First-tr, FPtr around each of next 3 sts, ch 2, sk next 2 sts, *3/3 FPdtr LC, ch 2, sk next 2 sts; rep from * to last 4 sts, FPtr around each of next 3 sts 2 rows below, turn.

Row 6: Rep row 2.

Rep rows 3–6 for pattern st.

SPECIAL TECHNIQUES

End Cap Finishing Stitch (see Special Techniques, p. 108)
Locking Mattress Stitch (see Special Techniques, p. 104)

NOTE

Garment is made from cuff to cuff; first sleeve is made, then stitches are added for main body using Ext-Fsc sts; second sleeve is made by attaching new yarn and continuing in Woven Cables Lace pattern st.

INSTRUCTIONS

Garment Panel (make 2)

First Sleeve

Foundation Row: Work 66 (66, 66, 66, 74, 74, 74, 74) Fsc, turn.

Rows 1–26 (26, 26, 26, 26, 26, 30, 30): Work in Woven Cables Lace pattern st.

Row 27 (27, 31, 31): Rep row 3.

Sizes L (1X, 2X, 3X)

Rows 27–29: Rep rows 3–5.

Main Body

In the first row of this section, sc are worked across the existing sts, then Ext-Fsc sts are used to extend the row to the full body length.

Transition Row (WS): Ch 1, sc in each st across to end of row, do not turn; insert hook in last st worked, yo and draw up a loop, yo and draw through 1 loop (first "chain" made), yo and draw through 2 loops on hook (first Ext-Fsc made), [insert hook under 2 loops of the "chain" just made, yo and draw up a loop, yo and draw through 1 loop ("chain" made), yo and draw through 2 loops on hook (Ext-Fsc made)] 104 (104, 112, 112, 112, 112, 112) times, turn—170 (170, 178, 178, 186, 186, 186) sts.

Rows 1–54 (60, 66, 72, 78, 84, 90, 96): Work in Woven Cables Lace pattern st as established.

Cut yarn, leaving tail for weaving in; pull tail through last st made; weave in tail using End Cap Finishing Stitch.

Second Sleeve

With RS facing, sk first 104 (104, 112, 112, 112, 112, 112) sts on last row worked, join yarn in next st; first st of Second Sleeve row 1 is worked in same st as joining.

Rows 1–28 (28, 30, 30, 30, 30, 32, 32): Work in Woven Cables Lace pattern st.

Cut yarn, leaving tail for weaving in; pull tail through last st made; weave in tail using End Cap Finishing Stitch.

FINISHING

Block all pieces to measurements in schematic.
Using Locking Mattress Stitch sew seams as follows:
Sew shoulder seams leaving 7 (7, 8, 8, 9, 9.5, 10, 10)"/18 (18, 20.5, 20.5, 23, 24, 25.5, 25.5) cm for neckline.
Sew seams under sleeves and continue to sew seams along sides of main body.
Weave in all ends

T-top Schematic

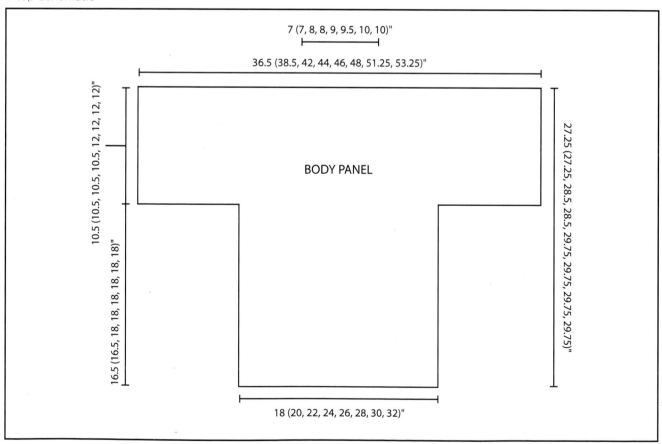

7 (7, 8, 8, 9, 9.5, 10, 10)"

36.5 (38.5, 42, 44, 46, 48, 51.25, 53.25)"

10.5 (10.5, 10.5, 10.5, 12, 12, 12, 12)"

BODY PANEL

27.25 (27.25, 28.5, 28.5, 29.75, 29.75, 29.75, 29.75)"

16.5 (16.5, 18, 18, 18, 18, 18, 18)"

18 (20, 22, 24, 26, 28, 30, 32)"

CIRCLE T-TOP

Strictly speaking, the geometric basis of this top consists of a semicircle and two rectangles stacked one atop the other like a set of building blocks. But really all that matters is that your humble T-top has never looked better with radiating center lines and a light lace stitch pattern that is quick and easy to stitch up. You'll love making this one as much as you love wearing it

SKILL LEVEL: ◖◼◼◼▭
Intermediate

SIZES: S (M, L, XL, 2X, 3X, 4X, 5X)
Samples shown in size small and 3X

FINISHED MEASUREMENTS

To Fit Bust: 32 (36, 40, 44, 48, 52, 56, 60)"/81.5 (91.5, 101.5, 112, 122, 132, 142, 152.5) cm

Finished Bust: 36 (40, 44, 48, 52, 56, 60, 64)"/91.5 (101.5, 112, 122, 132, 142, 152.5, 162.5) cm

Finished Length from Shoulder: 28 (28, 28.5, 29, 29, 29, 29.5, 29.5)"/71 (71, 72.5, 73.5, 73.5, 73.5, 75, 75) cm

MATERIALS AND TOOLS

Sample uses Malabrigo, Sock (100% superwash merino wool; 3.5 ounces/100 g = 440 yards/402 m): 3 (4, 4, 4, 5, 5, 5, 6) skeins; sample size small shown in color Tiziano Red #SW800; sample size 3X shown in color Solis #SW809—1320 (1760, 1760, 1760, 2200, 2200, 2200, 2640) yards/1208 (1610, 1610, 1610, 2012, 2012, 2012, 2415) m of superfine-weight yarn
Crochet hooks: 3.25 mm (size D-3) or size to obtain gauge
Yarn needle
Stitch markers

BLOCKED GAUGE

Double crochet fan: 5.6 sts = 1"/2.5 cm; 42 sts = 7.5"/19 cm; 2.3 rows = 1"/2.5 cm; 13 rows = 5.5"/14 cm

STITCH GUIDE

Foundation single crochet (Fsc): Ch 2, insert hook in 2nd ch from hook, yo and draw up a loop, yo and draw through 1 loop (first "chain" made), yo and draw through 2 loops on hook (first Fsc made), *insert hook under 2 loops of the "chain" just made, yo and draw up a loop, yo and draw through 1 loop ("chain" made), yo and draw through 2 loops on hook (Fsc made); rep from * for indicated number of foundation sts.

First double crochet (First-dc): Sc in first st, ch 2. *Note:* Use this st whenever the first st of a row is a dc. When working back in the First-dc at the end of the following row, insert hook into the second ch of the ch-2.

Double crochet fan (dc-fan): (2 dc, ch 1, 2 dc) in indicated st or sp.

Double crochet V-stitch (Dc-V): (Dc, ch 1, dc) in indicated st or sp.

PATTERN STITCHES

Double crochet fan (dc-fan) (worked on a multiple of 5 + 2 sts)

Swatch: 42 sts and 13 rows (+1 Fsc row)

Foundation Row: Work 42 Fsc, turn,

Row 1: First-dc, sk next 2 sts, dc-fan in next st, *ch 1, sk next 4 sts, dc-fan in next st; rep from * to last 3 sts, sk next 2 sts, dc in last st, turn.

Row 2: First-dc, dc-fan in ch-1 sp of next dc-fan, *ch 1, dc-fan in ch-1 sp of next dc-fan; rep from * to last st, dc in last st, turn.

Rep row 2 for pattern st.

Double crochet V-stitch half round (Dc-V Half Round)

Row 1: Dc 9 times in next st (place marker in first and last dc made).

Row 2: Dc-V in next st, [ch 1, sk next st, Dc-V in next st] 4 times.

Row 3: Dc-fan in ch-1 sp of next Dc-V, [ch 1, sk next ch-1 sp, dc-fan in ch-1 sp of next Dc-V] 4 times.

Row 4: Dc-fan in ch-1 sp of next Dc-V, [ch 1, Dc-V in ch-1 sp between dc-fans, ch 1, dc-fan in ch-1 sp of next dc-fan] 4 times.

Row 5: Dc-fan in ch-1 sp of next dc-fan, [ch 1, Dc-V in ch-1 sp of next Dc-V, ch 1, dc-fan in ch-1 sp of next dc-fan] 4 times.

Row 6: Dc-fan in ch-1 sp of next dc-fan, [ch 1, dc-fan in ch-1 sp of next Dc-V, ch 1, dc-fan in ch-1 sp of next dc-fan] 4 times.

Rows 7 and 8: Dc-fan in ch-1 sp of next dc-fan, [ch 1, dc-fan in ch-1 sp of next dc-fan] 8 times.

Row 9: Dc-fan in ch-1 sp of next dc-fan, [ch 1, dc in ch-1 sp between dc-fans, ch 1, dc-fan in ch-1 sp of next dc-fan] 8 times.

Row 10: Dc-fan in ch-1 sp of next dc-fan, [ch 1, sk next ch-1 sp, Dc-V in next st, ch 1, sk next ch-1 sp, dc-fan in ch-1 sp of next dc-fan] 8 times.

Row 11: Dc-fan in ch-1 sp of next dc-fan, [ch 1, Dc-V in ch-1 sp of next Dc-V, ch 1, dc-fan in ch-1 sp of next dc-fan] 8 times.

Row 12: Dc-fan in ch-1 sp of next dc-fan, [ch 1, dc-fan in ch-1 sp of next Dc-V, ch 1, dc-fan in ch-1 sp of next dc-fan] 8 times.

Rows 13 and 14: Dc-fan in ch-1 sp of next dc-fan, [ch 1, dc-fan in ch-1 sp of next dc-fan] 16 times.

Row 15: Dc-fan in ch-1 sp of next dc-fan, [ch 1, dc in ch-1 sp between dc-fans, ch 1, dc-fan in ch-1 sp of next dc-fan] 16 times.

Rows 16 and 17: Dc-fan in ch-1 sp of next dc-fan, [ch 1, sk next ch-1 sp, dc in next st, ch 1, sk next ch-1 sp, dc-fan in ch-1 sp of next dc-fan] 16 times.

Row 18: Dc-fan in ch-1 sp of next dc-fan, [ch 1, sk next ch-1 sp, Dc-V in next st, ch 1, sk next ch-1 sp, dc-fan in ch-1 sp of next dc-fan] 16 times.

Dc-fan

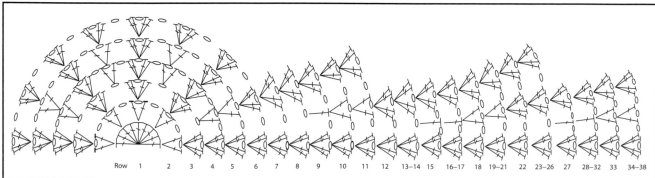

Rows 19–21: Dc-fan in ch-1 sp of next dc-fan, [ch 1, Dc-V in ch-1 sp of next Dc-V, ch 1, dc-fan in ch-1 sp of next dc-fan] 16 times.

Row 22: Dc-fan in ch-1 sp of next dc-fan, [ch 1, dc-fan in ch-1 sp of next Dc-V, ch 1, dc-fan in ch-1 sp of next dc-fan] 16 times.

Rows 23–26: Dc-fan in ch-1 sp of next dc-fan, [ch 1, dc-fan in ch-1 sp of next dc-fan] 32 times.

Row 27: Dc-fan in ch-1 sp of next dc-fan, [ch 1, dc in ch-1 sp between dc-fans, ch 1, dc-fan in ch-1 sp of next dc-fan] 32 times.

Rows 28–32: Dc-fan in ch-1 sp of next dc-fan, [ch 1, sk next ch-1 sp, dc in next st, ch 1, sk next ch-1 sp, dc-fan in ch-1 sp of next dc-fan] 32 times.

Row 33: Dc-fan in ch-1 sp of next dc-fan, [ch 1, sk next ch-1 sp, Dc-V in next st, ch 1, sk next ch-1 sp, dc-fan in ch-1 sp of next dc-fan] 32 times.

Rows 34–38: Dc-fan in ch-1 sp of next dc-fan, [ch 1, Dc-V in ch-1 sp of next Dc-V, ch 1, dc-fan in ch-1 sp of next dc-fan] 32 times.

SPECIAL TECHNIQUES

Knotless Starting Chain (see Special Techniques, p. 103)
End Cap Finishing Stitch (see Special Techniques, p. 108)
Locking Mattress Stitch (see Special Techniques, p. 104)

NOTES

1. Main body is worked in one piece from the center out with row 1 worked in both sides of the Foundation Row.

2. Main body is worked outward to beginning of sleeves. First sleeve is made by continuing on one side of garment with shortened rows. Second sleeve is made by attaching new yarn to opposite side of main body and working rows to match first sleeve.

INSTRUCTIONS

Body Panel (make 2)

Foundation Row: Work 92 (92, 97, 97, 102, 102, 107, 107) Fsc, turn.

Row 1: First-dc, sk next 2 sts, dc-fan in next st, *ch 1, sk next 4 sts, dc-fan in next st; rep from * to last 3 sts, sk next 2 sts, work row 1 of Dc-V Half Round pattern st, (now working in opposite side of Foundation Row), sk next 2 sts, dc-fan in next st, **ch 1, sk next 4 sts, dc-fan in next st; rep from ** to last 3 sts, sk next 2 sts, dc in last st, turn.

Row 2: First-dc, dc-fan in ch-1 sp of next dc-fan, *ch 1, dc-fan in ch-1 sp of next dc-fan; rep from * to first marker, work row 2 of Dc-V Half Round pattern st, **ch 1, dc-fan in ch-1 sp of next dc-fan; rep from ** to last st, dc in last st, turn.

Row 3: First-dc, dc-fan in ch-1 sp of next dc-fan, *ch 1, dc-fan in ch-1 sp of next dc-fan; rep from * to marker, work row 3 of Dc-V Half Round pattern st, **ch 1, dc-fan in ch-1 sp of next dc-fan; rep from ** to last st, dc in last st, turn.

Row 4: First-dc, dc-fan in ch-1 sp of next dc-fan, *ch 1, dc-fan in ch-1 sp of next dc-fan; rep from * to marker, work row 4 of Dc-V Half Round pattern st, **ch 1, dc-fan in ch-1 sp of next dc-fan; rep from ** to last st, dc in last st, turn.

Rows 5–21 (24, 26, 28, 31, 33, 35, 38): Continue to work in dc-fan pattern st as established and working corresponding rows of Dc-V Half Round pattern st.

Do not cut yarn at end of last row. Turn work and continue with First Sleeve instructions.

Begin First Sleeve

After turning work, place marker in any stitch on facing side of fabric. This will remind you which side to have facing when you begin working the Second Sleeve.

Row 1: First-dc, dc-fan in ch-1 sp of next dc-fan, [ch 1, dc-fan in ch-1 sp of next dc-fan] 10 (10, 11, 11, 12, 12, 13, 13) times, dc in next ch-1 sp between dc-fans, turn.

Row 2: First-dc, dc-fan in ch-1 sp of next dc-fan, *ch 1, dc-fan in ch-1 sp of next dc-fan; rep from * to last st, dc in last st, turn.

Rows 3–23 (23, 23, 23, 23, 24, 25, 25): Rep row 2.

Cut yarn, leaving tail for weaving in; pull tail through last st made; weave in using End Cap Finishing Stitch.

Begin Second Sleeve

Turn work so side with marker attached is facing. Join yarn in ch-1 sp opposite ch-1 sp used at bottom of First Sleeve. First st of row 1 of Second Sleeve is made in same sp as joining.

Row 1: First-dc, dc-fan in ch-1 sp of next dc-fan, [ch 1, dc-fan in ch-1 sp of next dc-fan] 10 (10, 11, 11, 12, 12, 13, 13) times, dc in next ch-1 sp between dc-fans, turn.

Row 2: First-dc, dc-fan in ch-1 sp of next dc-fan, *ch 1, dc-fan in ch-1 sp of next dc-fan; rep from * to last st, dc in last st, turn.

Rows 3–23 (23, 23, 23, 24, 25, 25): Rep row 2.

Cut yarn, leaving tail for weaving in; pull tail through last st made; weave in using End Cap Finishing Stitch.

FINISHING

Block all pieces to schematic measurements. Using Locking Mattress stitch, sew top of sleeve and shoulder seams, leaving 8 (8, 9, 9, 10, 10.5, 11, 11)"/20.5 (20.5, 23, 23, 25.5, 26.5, 28, 28) cm opening for neckline. Sew bottom of sleeves and continue to sew side seam approximately 6.5"/16.5 cm down from bottom of armhole. Weave in all ends.

Circle T-top Schematic

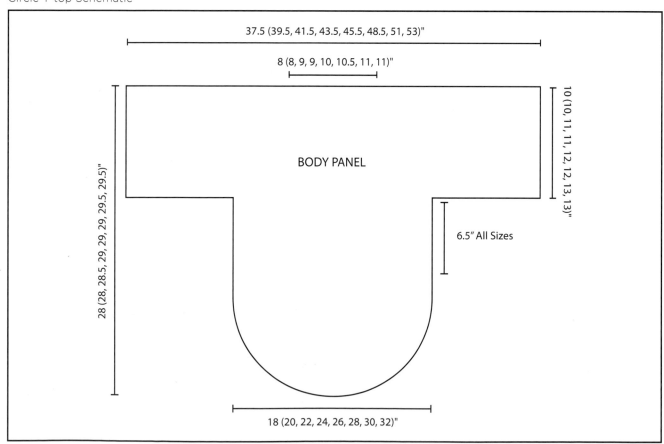

37.5 (39.5, 41.5, 43.5, 45.5, 48.5, 51, 53)"

8 (8, 9, 9, 10, 10.5, 11, 11)"

10 (10, 11, 11, 12, 12, 13, 13)"

BODY PANEL

28 (28, 28.5, 29, 29, 29, 29.5, 29.5)"

6.5" All Sizes

18 (20, 22, 24, 26, 28, 30, 32)"

RECTANGLES TOP

All rectangles all the time! This top is made up of seven rectangles of various sizes and two textures that come together flawlessly to create one chic top. Oversized proportions and dramatic ripple-ribbing on the removable cowl make this a statement piece that you will be proud to wear . . . and you'll look oh so stylish!

SKILL LEVEL: ◖■□◗
Easy

SIZES: S (M, L, XL, 2X, 3X, 4X, 5X)
Sample shown in size small

FINISHED MEASUREMENTS

To Fit Bust: 32 (36, 40, 44, 48, 52, 56, 60)"/81.5 (91.5, 101.5, 112, 122, 132, 142, 152.5) cm

Finished Length from Shoulder: 23 (23.25, 23.5, 24, 24, 24, 24.5, 24.5)"/58.5 (59, 59.5, 61, 61, 61, 62, 62) cm

MATERIALS AND TOOLS

Sample uses Malabrigo, Rios (100% superwash merino wool; 3.5 ounces/100 g = 210 yards/192 m): 11 (12, 14, 15, 16, 17, 19, 20) hanks in color Ravelry Red #611—2310 (2520, 2940, 3150, 3360, 3570, 3990, 4200) yards/2113 (2305, 2689, 2881, 3073, 3265, 3649, 3841) m of worsted-weight yarn

Crochet hooks: 4.00 mm (size G-6) and 4.50 mm (size 7) or sizes to obtain gauge

Yarn needle

Shown with 3, 1" and 2, 1.5" Flame Pedestal Buttons by JUL Designs

BLOCKED GAUGES

Single crochet linen stitch variation #1: 4.76 sts = 1"/2.5 cm; 25 sts = 5.25"/13 cm; 4.47 rows = 1"/2.5 cm; 19 rows = 4.25"/11 cm with larger hook

Single crochet ribbing: 4.8 sts = 1"/2.5 cm; 30 sts = 6.25"/16 cm; 4.7 rows = 1"/2.5 cm; 27 rows = 5.75"/14.5 cm with smaller hook

Single crochet ripple ribbing: 5.625 sts = 1"/2.5 cm; 45 sts = 8"/20.5cm; 4.44 rows = 1"/2.5 cm; 20 rows = 4.5"/11.5 cm with smaller hook

STITCH GUIDE

Foundation single crochet (Fsc): Ch 2, insert hook in 2nd ch from hook, yo and draw up a loop, yo and draw through 1 loop (first "chain" made), yo and draw through 2 loops on hook (first Fsc made), *insert hook under 2 loops of the "chain" just made, yo and draw up a loop, yo and draw through 1 loop ("chain" made), yo and draw through 2 loops on hook (Fsc made); rep from * for indicated number of foundation sts.

Single crochet through back loop only (sc-tbl): Insert hook in back loop of indicated st, yo and draw up a loop, yo and draw through 2 loops on hook.

PATTERN STITCHES

Single crochet linen stitch variation #1 (sc linen st var #1) (worked on a multiple of 2 + 1 sts)

Swatch: 25 sts and 18 rows (+1 Fsc row)

Foundation Row: With larger hook, work 25 Fsc, turn.

Row 1 (RS): Ch 1, sc in first st, *ch 1, sk next st, sc in next st; rep from * across, turn.

Row 2: Ch 1, sc in first st, *ch 1, sk next ch-1 sp, sc in next st; rep from * across, turn.

Rep row 2 for pattern st.

Single crochet ribbing (sc ribbing)

Swatch: 30 sts and 26 rows (+1 Fsc row)

Foundation Row: With smaller hook, work 30 Fsc, turn.

Row 1: Ch 1, sc in first st, sc-tbl in each st to last st, sc in last st, turn.

Rep row 1 for pattern st.

Single crochet ripple ribbing (sc ripple ribbing) (worked on a multiple of 15 sts)

Swatch: 45 sts and 19 rows (+1 Fsc row)

Foundation Row: With smaller hook, work 45 Fsc, turn.

Row 1: Ch 1, 2 sc in both loops of first st, sc-tbl in each of next 5 sts, [sk next st, sc-tbl in next st] 2 times, sc-tbl in each of next 4 sts, sc-tbl 2 times in next st, *sc-tbl 2 times in next st, sc-tbl in each of next 5 sts, [sk next st, sc-tbl in next st] 2 times, sc-tbl in each of next 4 sts, sc-tbl 2 times in next st; rep from * across to last 16 sts, sc-tbl 2 times in next st, sc-tbl in each of next 5 sts, [sk next st, sc-tbl in next st] 2 times, sc-tbl in each of next 4 sts, sc in both loops of last st, turn.

Row 2: Ch 1, sc in both loops of first st, sc-tbl in each st across to last st, sc in both loops of last st, turn.

Rep rows 1 and 2 for pattern st.

SPECIAL TECHNIQUES

End Cap Finishing Stitch (see Special Techniques, p. 108)
Locking Mattress Stitch (see Special Techniques, p. 104)

NOTE

Garment is made of rectangles made separately, then blocked and assembled according to finishing instructions.

Sc ribbing

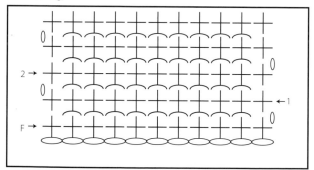

Sc linen st var #1

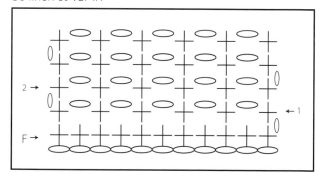

Sc ripple ribbing

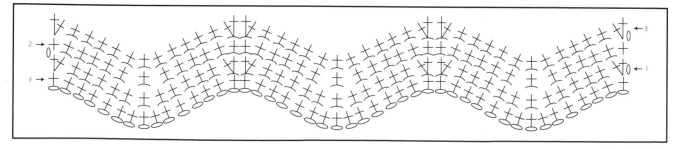

INSTRUCTIONS

Main Body Panel (make 2)

Foundation Row: With larger hook, work 181 (191, 205, 215, 229, 239, 249, 259) Fsc, turn.

Rows 1–76 (77, 78, 80, 81, 81, 83, 83): Work in sc linen st var #1 pattern st.

Cut yarn, leaving tail for weaving; pull tail through last st made; weave in tail using End Cap Finishing Stitch.

Cuff Ribbing (make 2)

Foundation Row: With smaller hook, work 15 Fsc, turn.

Rows 1–160 (162, 165, 167, 169, 169, 174, 174): Work in sc ribbing pattern st.

Cut yarn, leaving tail for weaving; pull tail through last st made; weave in tail using End Cap Finishing Stitch.

Bottom Ribbing

Foundation Row: With smaller hook, work 29 Fsc, turn.

Rows 1–170 (188, 207, 226, 244, 263, 282, 301): Work in sc ribbing pattern st.

Cut yarn, leaving tail for weaving; pull tail through last st made; weave in tail using End Cap Finishing Stitch.

Cowl

Foundation Row: With smaller hook, work 105 Fsc, turn.

Rows 1–156: Work in sc ripple ribbing pattern st.

Cut yarn, leaving tail for weaving; pull tail through last st made; weave in tail using End Cap Finishing Stitch.

FINISHING

Block all pieces to measurements in schematic.
Use Locking Mattress Stitch to sew pieces together as follows:
Sew shoulder seams at tops of Main Body Panels, leaving 9 (9, 10, 10, 11, 11, 12, 12)"/23 (23, 25.5, 25.5, 28, 28, 30.5, 30.5) cm for neckline opening.
Sew seams at either side of bottom of Main Body Panels as shown in schematic.
Sew long sides of Cuff Ribbing to outside edges of Main Body Panels.
Center Bottom Ribbing as shown in schematic. Pin center point of one long edge of Bottom Ribbing to left seam at bottom of Main Body Panel; pin corners of same long edge of Bottom Ribbing to right seam at bottom of Main Body Panel; place pins to evenly distribute Bottom Ribbing evenly around opening in bottom of Main Body Panel; sew Bottom Ribbing into place.
Fold Cowl in half lengthwise and sew three open sides closed.
When wearing Cowl, post buttons may be placed along overlapping and folded edge of Cowl. Post buttons may also be placed along side of bottom ribbing panel as shown or decorative buttons can be added for style points.
Weave in all ends.

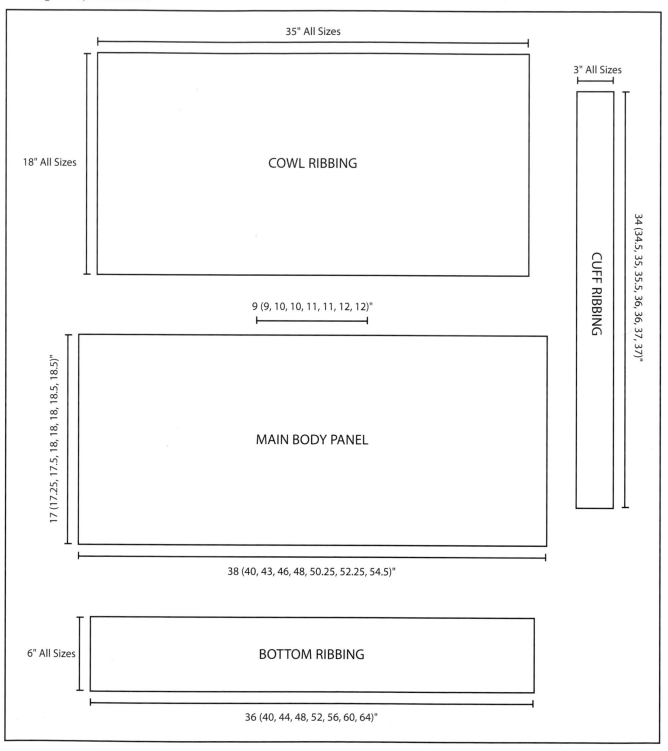

35" All Sizes

3" All Sizes

COWL RIBBING

18" All Sizes

34 (34.5, 35, 35.5, 36, 36, 37, 37)"

CUFF RIBBING

9 (9, 10, 10, 11, 11, 12, 12)"

17 (17.25, 17.5, 18, 18, 18.5, 18.5)"

MAIN BODY PANEL

38 (40, 43, 46, 48, 50.25, 52.25, 54.5)"

6" All Sizes

BOTTOM RIBBING

36 (40, 44, 48, 52, 56, 60, 64)"

GATHERED SHOULDER SLEEVELESS TOP

Once again we looked to rectangles as the building blocks for this elegant design. We mixed and matched lace and solid texture stitches to give a bit of flare in the back, while the subtle drape of the front is created with a simple play on dimensions. Gathering the finished shoulder seams creates gentle folds along the tops of the front panel. You'll love the fit and feel of this top whether you wear it as a stand-alone piece or layer it under your favorite jacket.

SKILL LEVEL: ⬛⬛☐☐
Easy

SIZES: S (M, L, XL, 2X, 3X, 4X, 5X)
Sample shown in size small

FINISHED MEASUREMENTS
To Fit Bust: 32 (36, 40, 44, 48, 52, 56, 60)"/81.5 (91.5, 101.5, 112, 122, 132, 142, 152.5) cm
Finished Bust: 35 (39.5, 43.3, 48.25, 52.3, 56, 60.25, 64)"/89 (100.5, 110, 122.5, 133, 142, 153, 162.5) cm
Finished Length from Shoulder: 25 (25, 25.5, 26, 26, 26, 26.5, 26.5)"/63.5 (63.5, 65, 66, 66, 66, 67.5, 67.5) cm

MATERIALS AND TOOLS

Sample uses Mango Moon, Mulberry Meadow (75% superwash merino/25% mulberry silk; 1.75 ounces/50 g = 218 yards/199 m): 5 (6, 6, 7, 7, 8, 9, 9) balls in color Lupine #5604—1090 (1308, 1308, 1526, 1526, 1744, 1962, 1962) yards/ 997 (1197, 1197, 1396, 1396, 1595, 1795, 1795) m of superfine-weight yarn
Crochet hook: 2.75 mm (size C-2) or size to obtain gauge
Yarn needle

BLOCKED GAUGES
Single crochet linen stitch variation #2: 7.375 sts = 1"/2.5 cm; 59 sts = 8"/20.5 cm; 6.17 rows = 1"/2.5 cm; 37 rows = 6"/15 cm
Double crochet V-stitch and fans: 7.18 sts = 1"/2.5 cm; 61 sts = 8.5"/21.5 cm; 4 rows = 1"/2.5 cm; 28 rows = 7"/18 cm

STITCH GUIDE

3-double crochet fan (3-dc fan): Dc 3 times in indicated st or sp.

First double crochet (First-dc): Sc in first st, ch 2. *Note:* Use this st whenever the first st of a row is a dc. When working back in the First-dc at the end of the following row, insert hook in to the second ch of the ch-2.

Double crochet V-stitch (Dc-V): (Dc, ch 1, dc) in indicated st or sp.

Single crochet through front loop only (sc-tfl): Insert hook in front loop of indicated st, yo and draw up a loop, yo and draw through 2 loops on hook.

PATTERN STITCHES

Single crochet linen stitch variation #2 (sc linen st var #2) (worked on a multiple of 2 + 1 sts)

Swatch: 59 sts and 36 rows (+1 Fsc row)

Foundation Rows: Work 59 Fsc, turn.

Row 1: Ch 1, sc in first st, ch 1, sk next st, *sc-tfl in next st, ch 1; rep from * to last st, sc in last st, turn.

Row 2: Ch 1, sc in first st, ch 1, sk next ch-1 sp, *sc-tfl in next st, ch 1; rep from * to last st, sc in last st, turn.

Rep row 2 for pattern st.

Double crochet V-stitch and fans (Dc-V and Fans) (worked on a multiple of 6 + 1 sts)

Swatch: 61 sts and 28 rows (+1 Fsc row)

Foundation Row: Work 61 Fsc, turn.

Row 1 (RS): Ch 1, sc in first st, *ch 1, sk next 2 sts, 3-dc fan in next st, ch 1, sk next 2 sts, sc in next st; rep from * to end of row, turn.

Row 2: (First-dc, dc) in first st, ch 1, sc in center dc of next dc-fan, *ch 1, Dc-V in next sc, ch 1, sc in center dc of next 3-dc fan; rep from * to last sc, ch 1, dc 2 times in last sc, turn.

Row 3: Ch 1, sc in first st, ch 1, 3-dc fan in next sc, ch 1, *sc in ch-1 sp of next Dc-V, ch 1, 3-dc fan in next sc, ch 1; rep from * to last 2 dc, sk next dc, sc in last st, turn.

Rep rows 2 and 3 for pattern st.

SPECIAL TECHNIQUES

End Cap Finishing Stitch (see Special Techniques, p. 108)
Locking Mattress Stitch (see Special Techniques, p. 104)

Sc linen st var #2

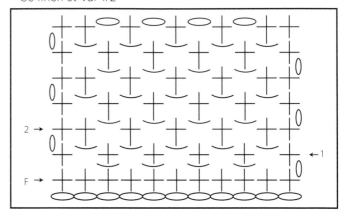

Dc-V and Fans

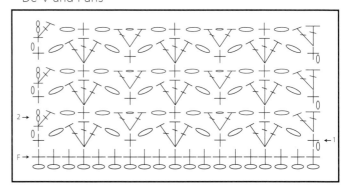

Gathered Shoulder Sleeveless Top Schematic

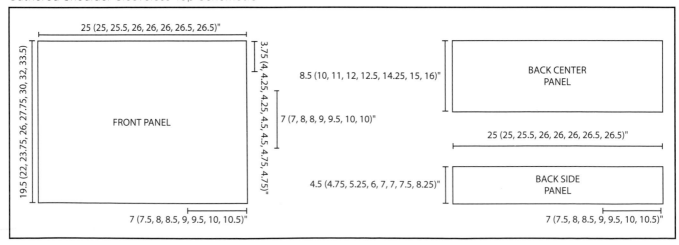

NOTE

Drape in front of garment is created by making a front panel that is 2"/5 cm wider than the back panel, then sewing the outside edges of the front panel to the outside edges of the back panel.

INSTRUCTIONS

Front Panel

Foundation Row: Work 143 (161, 175, 191, 205, 221, 235, 247) Fsc, turn.

Rows 1–155 (155, 158, 161, 161, 161, 164, 164): Work in sc linen st var #2 pattern st.

Cut yarn, leaving tail for weaving in; pull tail through last st made; weave in using End Cap Finishing Stitch.

Back Side Panel (make 2)

Foundation Row: Work 33 (35, 39, 45, 51, 51, 56, 61) Fsc, turn.

Rows 1–155 (155, 158, 161, 161, 161, 164, 164): Work in sc linen st var #2 pattern st.

Cut yarn, leaving tail for weaving in; pull tail through last st made; weave in using End Cap Finishing Stitch.

Back Center Panel

Foundation Row: Work 61 (73, 79, 85, 91, 103, 109, 115) Fsc, turn.

Rows 1–100 (100, 102, 104, 104, 104, 106, 106): Work Dc-V and Fans pattern st.

Cut yarn, leaving tail for weaving in; pull tail through last st made; weave in using End Cap Finishing Stitch.

FINISHING

Block all pieces to measurements in schematic.
Using Locking Mattress Stitch, assemble garment as follows:
Sew Back Side Panels to Back Center Panel.
Match Front Panel top outside corners to assembled Back Panel outside corners and pin into place. Starting from pinned outside corners, sew 3.75 (4, 4.25, 4.25, 4.5, 4.5, 4.75, 4.75)"/9.5 (10, 10, 11, 11.5, 11.5, 12, 12) cm shoulder seams.
Sew side seams leaving 7 (7.5, 8, 8.5, 9, 9.5, 10, 10.5)"/18 (19, 20.5, 21.5, 23, 24, 25.5, 26.5) cm for armholes.
Shoulder gathers: thread one end of a length of yarn through yarn needle, loosely weave half of yarn length along sewn shoulder seam; now thread other end of length of same yarn through yarn needle, loosely weave other half of yarn length along sewn shoulder seam ending in same spot as first woven end; now gently pull both loose ends of yarn creating gathers along shoulder seam as shown in photos. Secure loose ends of yarn and weave in.
Weave in all ends.

COWL NECK TUNIC

This cozy yet chic tunic is comprised of a simple and elegant application of rectangles made in complementary texture stitches that give subtle shaping and definition to the finished piece. Two rectangles for the main body, one rectangle for the cowl neckline, and you're done! Treat yourself to the long lines of this figure flattering design and see just how amazing you'll look and feel.

SKILL LEVEL: ▮▮▯▯ Easy

SIZES: S (M, L, XL, 2X, 3X, 4X, 5X)
Sample shown in size small

FINISHED MEASUREMENTS

To Fit Bust: 32 (36, 40, 44, 48, 52, 56, 60)"/81.5 (91.5, 101.5, 112, 122, 132, 142, 152.5) cm

Finished Bust: 36 (40, 44.5, 48.25, 53, 57, 61.5, 65.25)" /91.5 (101.5, 113, 122.5, 134.5, 145, 156, 165.5) cm

Finished Hip: 36.25 (40.25, 45.5, 49.5, 53.25, 57.25, 61.25, 65)"/92 (102, 115, 123.5, 135.5, 145.5, 155.5, 165) cm

Finished Length from Shoulder: 30.25 (30.25, 30.75, 32, 32, 33, 33.5, 33.5)"/77 (77, 78, 81.5, 81.5, 84, 85, 85) cm

MATERIALS AND TOOLS

Sample uses Cascade, Heritage (75% superwash merino wool, 25% nylon; 3.5 ounces/100 g per hank = 437 yards/399.6 m): 5 (6, 6, 7, 8, 8, 9, 9) hanks in color Sapphire #5636—2185 (2622, 2622, 3059, 3496, 3496, 3933, 3933) yards/ 1998 (2398, 2398, 2798, 3197, 3197, 3597, 3597) m of superfine-weight yarn

Crochet hook: 2.75 mm (size C-2) or size to obtain gauge

Yarn needle

BLOCKED GAUGES

Single crochet V-stitch: 7.78 sts = 1"/2.5 cm; 35 sts = 4.5"/11.5 cm; 5.33 rows = 1"/2.5 cm; 20 rows = 3.75"/9.5 cm

Single crochet V-stitch variation #1: 7.65 sts = 1"/2.5 cm; 44 sts = 5.75"/14.5 cm; 5.18 rows = 1"/2.5 cm; 22 rows = 4.25"/11 cm

Single crochet V-stitch variation #2: 7.48 sts = 1"/2.5 cm; 43 sts = 5.75"/14.5 cm; 5.18 rows = 1"/2.5 cm; 22 rows = 4.25"/11 cm

STITCH GUIDE

Foundation single crochet (Fsc): Ch 2, insert hook in 2nd ch from hook, yo and draw up a loop, yo and draw through 1 loop (first "chain" made), yo and draw through 2 loops on hook (first Fsc made), *insert hook under 2 loops of the "chain" just made, yo and draw up a loop, yo and draw through 1 loop ("chain" made), yo and draw through 2 loops on hook (Fsc made); rep from * for indicated number of foundation sts.

Single crochet V-stitch (Sc-V): (Sc, ch 2, sc) in indicated st or sp.

Single crochet 2 together (sc2tog): Insert hook in next st and pull up a loop, insert hook in next st and pull up a loop, yarn over and draw through all 3 loops on hook.

PATTERN STITCHES

Single crochet V-stitch (Sc-V) (worked on a multiple of 3 + 2 sts)

Swatch: 35 sts and 20 rows (+1 Fsc row)

Foundation Row: Work 35 Fsc, turn.

Row 1: Ch 1, sc in first st, sk next st, Sc-V in next st, *sk next 2 sts, Sc-V in next st; rep from * to last 2 sts, sk next st, sc in last st, turn.

Row 2: Ch 1, sc in first st, Sc-V in ch-2 sp of each Sc-V across row, sc in last st, turn.

Rep row 2 for pattern st.

Single crochet V-stitch variation #1 (Sc-V var #1) (worked on a multiple of 5 + 4 sts)

Swatch: 44 sts and 22 rows (+1 Fsc row)

Foundation Row: Work 44 Fsc, turn.

Row 1: Ch 1, sc in first st, ch 2, sk next 3 sts, *Sc-V in next st, ch 2, sk next 4 sts; rep from * to last st, sc in last st, turn.

Row 2: Ch 1, sc in first st, ch 2, *Sc-V in ch-2 sp of next Sc-V, ch 2; rep from * to last st, sc in last st, turn.

Rep row 2 for pattern st.

Single crochet V-stitch variation #2 (Sc-V var #2) (worked on a multiple of 4 + 3 sts)

Swatch: 43 sts and 22 rows (+1 Fsc row)

Foundation Row: Work 43 Fsc, turn.

Row 1: Ch 1, sc in first st, ch 1, sk next 2 sts, Sc-V in next st, ch 1, *sk next 3 sts, Sc-V in next st, ch 1; rep from * to last 3 sts, sk next 2 sts, sc in last st, turn.

Row 2: Ch 1, sc in first st, ch 1, *Sc-V in ch-2 sp of next Sc-V, ch 1; rep from * to last st, sc in last st, turn.

Rep row 2 for pattern st.

Sc-V

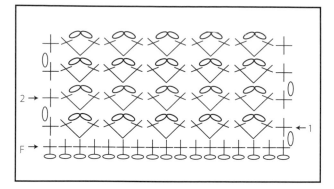

Sc-V var #1

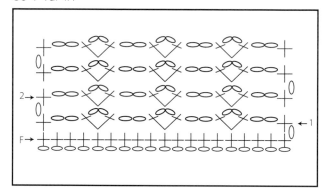

Sc-V var #2

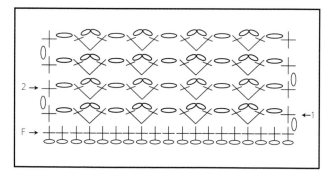

SPECIAL TECHNIQUES

End Cap Finishing Stitch (see Special Techniques, p. 108)
Locking Mattress Stitch (see Special Techniques, p. 104)

NOTE

Bottom Lace Panel is made first from the top down, then stitches for Main Body Panel are picked up in Foundation Row of Bottom Lace Panel. Main Body Panel is then made from bottom up to shoulders. Cowl Panel is made separately in one piece, then sewn to neckline after Main Body Panels are sewn together.

INSTRUCTIONS

Body Panel (make 2)

Bottom Lace Panel

Foundation Row: Work 139 (154, 174, 189, 204, 219, 234, 249) Fsc, turn.

Rows 1-37 (37, 37, 42, 42, 47, 47, 47): Work in Sc-V var #1 pattern st.

Cut yarn, leaving tail for weaving in; pull tail through last st made; weave in using End Cap Finishing Stitch.

Main Body Panel

With RS Facing, join yarn in bottom of first Fsc of Bottom Lace Panel; first st of Main Body Panel Transition Row is made in same st as joining.

Sizes S (M) Only

Transition Row: Ch 1, sc in first st, sc 2 times in next st, sc in next st and in each st to end of row, turn—140 (155) sts.

Sizes L (1X) Only

Transition Row: Ch 1, sc in first st, sc2tog, sc in next st and in each st to end of row, turn—173 (188) sts.

Sizes 2X (3X) Only

Transition Row: Ch 1, sc in first st, sc 2 times in next st, sc in next st and in each st to last 2 sts, sc 2 times in next st, sc in last st, turn—206 (221) sts.

Size 4X Only

Transition Row: Ch 1, sc in each of first 38 sts, sc 2 times in next st, [sc in each of next 38 sts, sc 2 times in next st] 4 times, sc in each of last 39 sts, turn—239 sts.

Size 5X Only

Transition Row: Ch 1, sc in each of first 40 sts, [sc 2 times in next st, sc in each of next 41 sts] 4 times, sc 2 times in next st, sc in each of last 40 sts, turn—254 sts.

All Sizes

Rows 1–123 (123, 126, 128, 128, 128, 131, 131): Work in Sc-V pattern st.

Cut yarn, leaving tail for weaving in; pull tail through last st made; weave in using End Cap Finishing Stitch.

Cowl Panel

Foundation Row: Work 227 (227, 227, 235, 235, 235, 239, 239) Fsc, turn.

Rows 1–47: Work in Sc-V var #2 pattern st.

Cut yarn, leaving tail for weaving in; pull tail through last st made; weave in using End Cap Finishing Stitch.

FINISHING

Block all pieces to measurements in schematic.
Using Locking Mattress Stitch, sew shoulder seams and side body seams. Sew Cowl Panel to neckline.
Gently block seams to even out.
Weave in all ends.

Cowl Neck Tunic Schematic

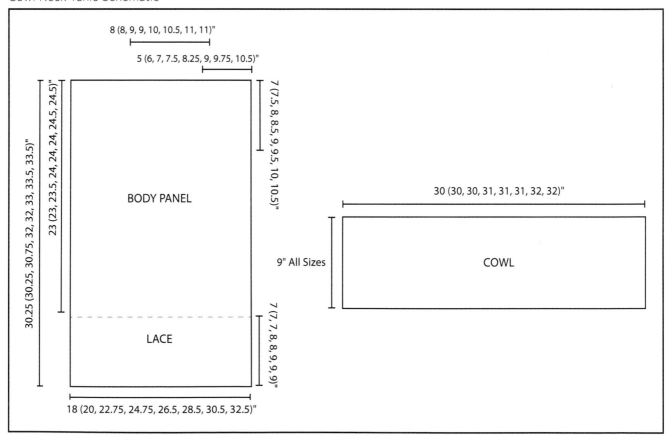

WRAPS

SPLIT CIRCLE WRAP

Dramatic lace vines traveling up columns bisect the circular vine motif into two congruent halves. You will be enthralled as you stitch, watching the vining half circles grow from the center point of the motif.

The sweeping curves of the front panels and flattering open folds of the neckline create a classic look adjustable for any body shape depending on where you place your front closures.

SKILL LEVEL: ⬛⬛⬛◻◻
Experienced

SIZES: S (M, L, XL, 2X, 3X, 4X, 5X)
Samples shown in size small and 3X

FINISHED MEASUREMENTS
To Fit Bust: 32 (36, 40, 44, 48, 52, 56, 60)"/81.5 (91.5, 101.5, 112, 122, 132, 142, 152.5) cm
Finished Bust: 37 (39.5, 44, 47, 53, 56.5, 60, 64.5)"/94 (100.5, 112, 119.5, 134.5, 143.5, 152.5, 164) cm

MATERIALS AND TOOLS

Sample uses Cascade, Longwood Sport (100% superwash extrafine merino wool; 3.5 ounces/100 g = 273 yards/250 m): 4 (4, 4, 5, 5, 6, 6, 6) skeins; sample size small shown in color Green Olive #15; sample size 3X shown in color Plum #28.—1092 (1092, 1092, 1365, 1365, 1638, 1638, 1638) yards/999 (999, 999, 1249, 1249, 1498, 1498, 1498) m sport-weight yarn
Crochet hook: 3.50 mm (size E-4) or size to obtain gauge
Yarn needle
Shown using Dayak and Wild Grape Tendril Shawl Pins by JUL Designs

BLOCKED GAUGES
Vines Center Panel: 4.56 sts = 1"/2.5 cm; 41 sts = 9"/23 cm; 2.06 rows = 1"/2.5 cm; 34 rows = 16.5"/42 cm
Vines Half Circle: 4 sts = 1"; 1.8 rows = 1"

STITCH GUIDE

Foundation single crochet (Fsc): Ch 2, insert hook in 2nd ch from hook, yo and draw up a loop, yo and draw through 1 loop (first "chain" made), yo and draw through 2 loops on hook (first Fsc made), * insert hook under 2 loops of the "chain" just made, yo and draw up a loop, yo and draw through 1 loop ("chain" made), yo and draw through 2 loops on hook (Fsc made); repeat from * for indicated number of foundation stitches.

First double crochet (First-dc): Sc in first st, ch 2. *Note:* Use this st whenever the first st of a row is a dc. When working back in the First-dc at the end of the following row, insert hook into the second ch of the ch-2.

First double crochet 2 together (First-dc2tog): Sc in first st, ch 1, yo, insert hook in next st, yo and draw up a loop, (yo and draw through 2 loops on hook) twice.

Double crochet 2 together (dc2tog): Yo, insert hook in indicated st or sp, yo and draw up a loop, yo and draw through 2 loops on hook, yo, insert hook in next st, yo and draw up a loop, yo and draw through 2 loops on hook, yo and draw through all 3 loops on hook.

Double crochet 3 together (dc3tog): Yo, insert hook in indicated st or sp, yo and draw up a loop, yo and draw through 2 loops on hook, (yo, insert hook in next st, yo and draw up a loop, yo and draw through 2 loops on hook) twice, yo and draw through all 4 loops on hook.

Double crochet fan (dc-fan): (2 dc, ch 2, 2 dc) in indicated st or sp.

PATTERN STITCH

Vines Center Panel (worked over 41 sts) (Chart on p. 77)

Row 1 (RS): Dc in each of next 11 sts, ch 3, sk next 4 sts, dc-fan in next st, ch 3, sk next 4 sts, dc in next st, ch 3, sk next 4 sts, dc-fan in next st, ch 3, sk next 4 sts, dc in each of next 11 sts.

Row 2: Dc in each of next 10 sts, ch 3, sk next st and next ch-3 sp, dc-fan in ch-2 sp of next dc-fan, ch 3, sk next ch-3 sp, dc 3 times in next st, ch 3, sk next ch-3 sp, dc-fan in ch-2 sp of next dc-fan, ch 3, sk next ch-3 sp and next st, dc in each of next 10 sts.

Row 3: Dc in each of next 8 sts, ch 3, sk next 2 sts and next ch-3 sp, dc-fan in ch-2 sp of next dc-fan, ch 3, sk next ch-3 sp, dc 3 times in next st, ch 3, sk next st, dc 3 times in next st, ch 3, sk next ch-3 sp, dc-fan in ch-2 sp of next dc-fan, ch 3, sk next ch-3 sp and next 2 sts, dc in each of next 8 sts.

Row 4: Dc in each of next 5 sts, ch 3, sk next 3 sts and next ch-3 sp, dc-fan in ch-2 sp of next dc-fan, ch 3, sk next ch-3 sp, dc 2 times in next st, dc in next st, dc 2 times in next st, ch 3, sk next ch-3 sp, dc 2 times in next st, dc in next st, dc 2 times in next st, ch 3, sk next ch-3 sp, dc-fan in ch-2 sp of next dc-fan, ch 3, sk next ch-3 sp and next 3 sts, dc in each of next 5 sts.

Row 5: Dc in each of next 3 sts, ch 3, sk next 2 sts and next ch-3 sp, dc-fan in ch-2 sp of next dc-fan, ch 3, sk next ch-3 sp, dc 2 times in next st, dc in each of next 3 sts, dc 2 times in next st, ch 3, sk next ch-3 sp, dc 2 times in next st, dc in each of next 3 sts, dc 2 times in next st, ch 3, sk next ch-3 sp, dc-fan in ch-2 sp of next dc-fan, ch 3, sk next ch-3 sp and next 2 sts, dc in each of next 3 sts.

Row 6: Dc in each of next 3 sts, ch 3, sk next ch-3 sp, dc-fan in ch-2 sp of next dc-fan, ch 3, sk next ch-3 sp, dc2tog, dc in each of next 3 sts, dc2tog, ch 3, sk next ch, dc in next ch, ch 3, sk next ch, dc2tog, dc in each of next 3 sts, dc2tog, ch 3, sk next ch-3 sp, dc-fan in ch-2 sp of next dc-fan, ch 3, sk next ch-3 sp, dc in each of next 3 sts.

Row 7: Dc in each of next 3 sts, ch 3, sk next ch-3 sp, dc-fan in ch-2 sp of next dc-fan, ch 3, sk next ch-3 sp, dc2tog, dc in next st, dc2tog, ch 3, sk next ch-3 sp, dc 3 times in next st, ch 3, sk next ch-3 sp, dc2tog, dc in next st, dc2tog, ch 3, sk next ch-3 sp, dc-fan in ch-2 sp of next dc-fan, ch 3, sk next ch-3 sp, dc in each of next 3 sts.

Row 8: Dc in each of next 3 sts, ch 3, sk next ch-3 sp, dc-fan in ch-2 sp of next dc-fan, ch 3, sk next ch-3 sp, dc3tog, ch 3, sk next ch-3 sp, dc 3 times in next st, ch 3, sk next st, dc 3 times in next st, ch 3, sk next ch-3 sp, dc3tog, ch 3, sk next ch-3 sp, dc-fan in ch-2 sp of next dc-fan, ch 3, sk next ch-3 sp, dc in each of next 3 sts.

Row 9: Dc in each of next 3 sts, ch 3, sk next ch-3 sp, dc-fan in ch-2 sp of next dc-fan, ch 3, sk next ch-3 sp, dc in next st, ch 3, sk next ch-3 sp, dc 2 times in next st, dc in next st, dc 2 times in next st, ch 3, sk next ch-3 sp, dc 2 times in next st, dc in next st, dc 2 times in next st, ch 3, sk next ch-3 sp, dc in next st, ch 3, sk next ch-3 sp, dc-fan in ch-2 sp of next dc-fan, ch 3, sk next ch-3 sp, dc in each of next 3 sts.

Row 10: Dc in each of next 3 sts, ch 3, sk next ch-3 sp, dc-fan in ch-2 sp of next dc-fan, ch 3, sk next ch-3 sp and next st and next ch-3 sp, dc 2 times in next st, dc in each of next 3 sts, dc 2 times in next st, ch 3, sk next ch-3 sp, dc 2 times in next st, dc in each of next 3 sts, dc 2 times in next st, ch 3, sk next ch-3 sp and next st and next ch-3 sp, dc-fan in ch-2 sp of next dc-fan, ch 3, sk next ch-3 sp, dc in each of next 3 sts.

Row 11: Dc in each of next 3 sts, ch 3, sk next ch-3 sp, dc-fan in ch-2 sp of next dc-fan, ch 3, sk next ch-3 sp, dc2tog, dc in each of next 3 sts, dc2tog, ch 3, sk next ch, dc in next ch, ch 3, sk next ch, dc2tog, dc in each of next 3 sts, dc2tog, ch 3, sk next ch-3 sp, dc-fan in ch-2 sp of next dc-fan, ch 3, sk next ch-3 sp, dc in each of next 3 sts.

Row 12: Dc in each of next 3 sts, dc in next ch, ch 3, sk next 2 chs, dc-fan in ch-2 sp of next dc-fan, ch 3, sk next ch-3 sp, dc2tog, dc in next st, dc2tog, ch 3, sk next ch-3 sp, dc 3 times in next st, ch 3, sk next ch-3 sp, dc2tog, dc in next st, dc2tog, ch 3, sk next ch-3 sp, dc-fan in ch-2 sp of next dc-fan, ch 3, sk next 2 chs, dc in next ch, dc in each of next 3 sts.

Row 13: Dc in each of next 4 sts, dc in next ch, ch 3, sk next 2 chs, dc-fan in ch-2 sp of next dc-fan, ch 3, sk next ch-3 sp, dc3tog, ch 3, sk next ch-3 sp, dc 2 times in next st, dc in next st, dc 2 times in next st, ch 3, sk next ch-3 sp, dc3tog, ch 3, sk next ch-3 sp, dc-fan in ch-2 sp of next dc-fan, ch 3, sk next 2 chs, dc in next ch, dc in each of next 4 sts.

Row 14: Dc in each of next 5 sts, dc in next ch, ch 3, sk next 2 chs, dc-fan in ch-2 sp of next dc-fan, ch 3, sk next ch-3 sp, dc in next st, ch 3, sk next ch-3 sp, dc 2 times in next st, dc in each of next 3 sts, dc 2 times in next st, ch 3, sk next ch-3 sp, dc in next st, ch 3, sk next ch-3 sp, dc-fan in ch-2 sp of next dc-fan, ch 3, sk next 2 chs, dc in next ch, dc in each of next 5 sts.

Row 15: Dc in each of next 6 sts, dc in each of next 3 chs, ch 3, dc-fan in ch-2 sp of next dc-fan, ch 3, sk next ch-3 sp and next st and next ch-3 sp, dc2tog, dc in each of next 3 sts, dc2tog, ch 3, sk next ch-3 sp and next st and next ch-3 sp, dc-fan in ch-2 sp of next dc-fan, ch 3, dc in each of next 3 chs, dc in each of next 6 sts.

Row 16: Dc in each of next 9 sts, dc in next ch, ch 3, sk next 2 chs, dc-fan in ch-2 sp of next dc-fan, ch 3, sk next ch-3 sp, dc2tog, dc in next st, dc2tog, ch 3, sk next ch-3 sp, dc-fan in ch-2 sp of next dc-fan, ch 3, sk next 2 chs, dc in next ch, dc in each of next 9 sts.

Row 17: Dc in each of next 10 sts, dc in next ch, ch 3, sk next 2 chs, dc-fan in ch-2 sp of next dc-fan, ch 3, sk next ch-3 sp, dc3tog, ch 3, sk next ch-3 sp, dc-fan in ch-2 sp of next dc-fan, ch 3, sk next 2 chs, dc in next ch, dc in each of next 10 sts.

Rep rows 1–17 for pattern st.

NOTE: To make a swatch for Vines Center Panel pattern stitch, work as follows:

Swatch: 41 sts and 34 rows (+1 Fsc row)

Foundation Row: Work 41 Fsc, turn.

Work 34 rows of Vines Center Panel pattern st replacing one dc at the beginning of each row with a first-dc. Turn at the end of each row.
Block finished swatch to 9" x 16.5".

SPECIAL TECHNIQUES
Knotless Starting Chain (see Special Techniques, p. 103)
End Cap Finishing Stitch (see Special Techniques, p. 108)
Duplicate Stitch (see Special Techniques, p. 105)
Locking Mattress Stitch (see Special Techniques, p. 104)

NOTES
1. Back Panel is made from the center out to the top and bottom using Foundation Row as the center point.
2. Front Panels are made as one half-circle motif, then sewn to Back Panel after blocking.

INSTRUCTIONS

Back Panel
First Half Back
Foundation Row: 84 (90, 100, 108, 120, 129, 137, 147) Fsc, turn.

Row 1 (RS): First-dc, dc in each of next 0 (3, 8, 12, 18, 2, 6, 11) sts, work row 1 of Vines Center Panel pattern st 2 (2, 2, 2, 2, 3, 3, 3) times, dc in each of next 1 (4, 9, 13, 19, 3, 7, 12) sts, turn.

Row 2: First-dc, dc in each of next 0 (3, 8, 12, 18, 2, 6, 11) sts, work row 2 of Vines Center Panel pattern st 2 (2, 2, 2, 2, 3, 3, 3) times, dc in each of next 1 (4, 9, 13, 19, 3, 7, 12) sts, turn.

Row 3: First-dc, dc in each of next 0 (3, 8, 12, 18, 2, 6, 11) sts, work row 3 of Vines Center Panel pattern st 2 (2, 2, 2, 2, 3, 3, 3) times, dc in each of next 1 (4, 9, 13, 19, 3, 7, 12) sts, turn.

Row 4: First-dc, dc in each of next 0 (3, 8, 12, 18, 2, 6, 11) sts, work row 4 of Vines Center Panel pattern st 2 (2, 2, 2, 2, 3, 3, 3) times, dc in each of next 1 (4, 9, 13, 19, 3, 7, 12) sts, turn.

Row 5: First-dc, dc in each of next 0 (3, 8, 12, 18, 2, 6, 11) sts, work row 5 of Vines Center Panel pattern st (2, 2, 2, 2, 3, 3, 3) times, dc in each of next 1 (4, 9, 13, 19, 3, 7, 12) sts, turn.

Row 6: First-dc, dc in each of next 0 (3, 8, 12, 18, 2, 6, 11) sts, work row 6 of Vines Center Panel pattern st (2, 2, 2, 2, 3, 3, 3) times, dc in each of next 1 (4, 9, 13, 19, 3, 7, 12) sts, turn.

Row 7: First-dc, dc in each of next 0 (3, 8, 12, 18, 2, 6, 11) sts, work row 7 of Vines Center Panel pattern st 2 (2, 2, 2, 2, 3, 3, 3) times, dc in each of next 1 (4, 9, 13, 19, 3, 7, 12) sts, turn.

Row 8: First-dc, dc in each of next 0 (3, 8, 12, 18, 2, 6, 11) sts, work row 8 of Vines Center Panel pattern st 2 (2, 2, 2, 2, 3, 3, 3) times, dc in each of next 1 (4, 9, 13, 19, 3, 7, 12) sts, turn.

Row 9: First dc, dc in each of next 0 (3, 8, 12, 18, 2, 6, 11) sts, work row 9 of Vines Center Panel pattern st 2 (2, 2, 2, 2, 3, 3, 3) times, dc in each of next 1 (4, 9, 13, 19, 3, 7, 12) sts, turn.

Row 10: First-dc, dc in each of next 0 (3, 8, 12, 18, 2, 6, 11) sts, work row 10 of Vines Center Panel pattern st 2 (2, 2, 2, 2, 3, 3, 3) times, dc in each of next 1 (4, 9, 13, 19, 3, 7, 12) sts, turn.

Rows 11–20 (20, 20, 20, 25, 30, 30, 35): Rep rows 6–10, 2 (2, 2, 2, 3, 4, 4, 5) times.

Row 21 (21, 21, 21, 26, 31, 31, 36): First-dc, dc in each of next 0 (3, 8, 12, 18, 2, 6, 11) sts, work row 11 of Vines Center Panel pattern st 2 (2, 2, 2, 2, 3, 3, 3) times, dc in each of next 1 (4, 9, 13, 19, 3, 7, 12) sts, turn.

Row 22 (22, 22, 22, 27, 32, 32, 37): First-dc, dc in each of next 0 (3, 8, 12, 18, 2, 6, 11) sts, work row 12 of Vines Center Panel pattern st 2 (2, 2, 2, 2, 3, 3, 3) times, dc in each of next 1 (4, 9, 13, 19, 3, 7, 12) sts, turn.

Row 23 (23, 23, 23, 28, 33, 33, 38): First-dc, dc in each of next 0 (3, 8, 12, 18, 2, 6, 11) sts, work row 13 of Vines Center Panel pattern st 2 (2, 2, 2, 2, 3, 3, 3) times, dc in each of next 1 (4, 9, 13, 19, 3, 7, 12) sts, turn.

Row 24 (24, 24, 24, 29, 34, 34, 39): First-dc, dc in each of next 0 (3, 8, 12, 18, 2, 6, 11) sts, work row 14 of Vines Center Panel pattern st 2 (2, 2, 2, 2, 3, 3, 3) times, dc in each of next 1 (4, 9, 13, 19, 3, 7, 12) sts, turn.

Row 25 (25, 25, 25, 30, 35, 35, 40): First-dc, dc in each of next 0 (3, 8, 12, 18, 2, 6, 11) sts, work row 15 of Vines Center Panel pattern st 2 (2, 2, 2, 2, 3, 3, 3) times, dc in each of next 1 (4, 9, 13, 19, 3, 7, 12) sts, turn.

Row 26 (26, 26, 26, 31, 36, 36, 41): First-dc, dc in each of next 0 (3, 8, 12, 18, 2, 6, 11) sts, work row 16 of Vines Center Panel pattern st 2 (2, 2, 2, 2, 3, 3, 3) times, dc in each of next 1 (4, 9, 13, 19, 3, 7, 12) sts, turn.

Row 27 (27, 27, 27, 32, 37, 37, 42): First-dc, dc in each of next 0 (3, 8, 12, 18, 2, 6, 11) sts, work row 17 of Vines Center Panel pattern st 2 (2, 2, 2, 2, 3, 3, 3) times, dc in each of next 1 (4, 9, 13, 19, 3, 7, 12) sts, turn.

Row 28 (28, 28, 28, 33, 38, 38, 43): First-dc, [dc in each st to next ch-3 sp, dc in each of next 3 chs, dc 3 times in ch-2 sp of next dc-fan, dc in each of next 3 chs, dc in next st, dc in each of next 3 chs, dc 3 times in ch-2 sp of next dc-fan, dc in each of next 11 sts] 2 (2, 2, 2, 3, 3, 3) times, dc in each st to end of row, turn.

Rows 29 (29, 29, 29, 34, 39, 39, 44)–(31, 33, 30, 38, 40, 43, 45): First-dc, dc in each st to end of row, turn.

Cut yarn, leaving tail for weaving in; pull tail through last st made; weave in tail using End Cap Finishing Stitch.

Second Half Back
With RS facing, join yarn in bottom of first st of Foundation Row; first st of row 1 is made in same st as joining.
Work as for First Half Back. (In other words, do exactly the same thing you did to make the First Half Back.)

Front Panel (make 2)
Row 1 (RS): (First-dc, dc 9 times) in Knotless Starting Chain, turn.

Split Circle Wrap Schematic

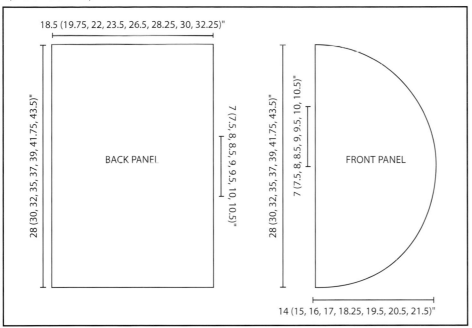

18.5 (19.75, 22, 23.5, 26.5, 28.25, 30, 32.25)"

28 (30, 32, 35, 37, 39, 41.75, 43.5)"

BACK PANEL

7 (7.5, 8, 8.5, 9, 9.5, 10, 10.5)"

28 (30, 32, 35, 37, 39, 41.75, 43.5)"

7 (7.5, 8, 8.5, 9, 9.5, 10, 10.5)"

FRONT PANEL

14 (15, 16, 17, 18.25, 19.5, 20.5, 21.5)"

Vines Center Panel Stitch

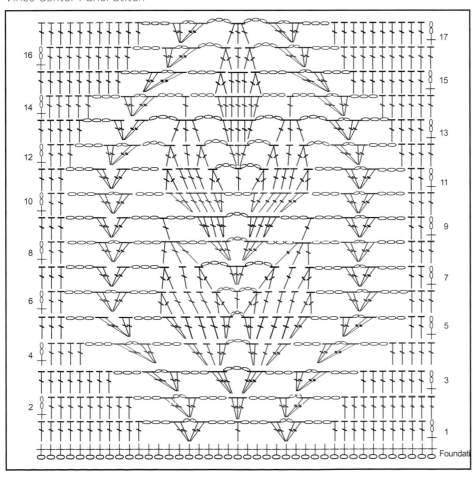

Row 36: First-dc, ch 2, sk next ch-2 sp, dc 2 times in next st, dc in next st, dc 2 times in next st, ch 1, sk next ch-3 sp, dc in next st, ch 1, sk next ch-3 sp, dc 2 times in next st, dc in next st, dc 2 times in next st, ch 3, sk next ch-3 sp, dc 2 times in next st, dc in next st, dc 2 times in next st, ch 3, sk next ch-1 sp, sk next dc, sk next ch-1 sp, dc 2 times in next st, dc in next of next 3 sts, dc 2 times in next st, ch 3, sk next ch-3 sp, dc 2 times in next st, dc in next of next 3 sts, dc 2 times in next st, ch 1, sk next ch-1 sp, sk next st, sk next ch-1 sp, dc in next st, ch 1, sk next ch-3 sp, [dc 2 times in next st, dc in next st, dc 2 times in next st, ch 3, sk next ch-3 sp, dc 2 times in next st, dc in next st, dc 2 times in next st, ch 1, sk next ch-3 sp, dc in next st, ch 1, sk next ch-3 sp, dc 2 times in next st, dc in next st, dc 2 times in next st, ch 3, sk next ch-3 sp, dc 2 times in next st, dc in next st, dc 2 times in next st, ch 3, sk next ch-1 sp, sk next dc, sk next ch-1 sp, dc 2 times in next st, dc in next of next 3 sts, dc 2 times in next st, ch 3, sk next ch-3 sp, dc 2 times in next st, dc in next of next 3 sts, dc 2 times in next st, ch 1, sk next ch-1 sp, sk next st, sk next ch-1 sp, dc in next st, ch 1, sk next ch-3 sp] 5 times, dc 2 times in next st, dc in next st, dc 2 times in next st, ch 2, sk next ch-2 sp, dc in last st, turn.

Row 37: First-dc, ch 2, sk next ch-2 sp, dc 2 times in next st, dc in each of next 3 sts, dc 2 times in next st, ch 3, sk next ch-1 sp, sk next st, sk next ch-1 sp, dc2tog, dc in each of next 3 sts, dc2tog, ch 3, sk next ch, dc in next ch, ch 3, sk next ch, dc2tog, dc in each of next 3 sts, dc2tog, ch 3, sk next ch-3 sp, dc 2 times in next st, dc in each of next 3 sts, dc 2 times in next st, ch 3, sk next ch-3 sp, dc 2 times in next st, dc in each of next 3 sts, dc 2 times in next st, ch 3, sk next ch-1 sp, sk next st, sk next ch-1 sp, [dc 2 times in next st, dc in each of next 3 sts, dc 2 times in next st, ch 3, sk next ch-3 sp, dc 2 times in next st, dc in each of next 3 sts, dc 2 times in next st, ch 3, sk next ch-1 sp, sk next st, sk next ch-1 sp, dc2tog, dc in each of next 3 sts, dc2tog, ch 3, sk next ch, dc in next ch, ch 3, sk next ch, dc2tog, dc in each of next 3 sts, dc2tog, ch 3, sk next ch-3 sp, dc 2 times in next st, dc in each of next 3 sts, dc 2 times in next st, ch 3, sk next ch-3 sp, dc 2 times in next st, dc in each of next 3 sts, dc 2 times in next st, ch 3, sk next ch-1 sp, sk next st, sk next ch-1 sp] 5 times, dc 2 times in next st, dc in each of next 3 sts, dc 2 times in next st, ch 2, sk next ch-2 sp, dc in last st, turn.

Cut yarn, leaving tail for weaving in; pull tail through last st made; weave in tail using End Cap Finishing Stitch.

Row 38: First-dc, ch 2, sk next ch-2 sp, dc2tog, dc in each of next 3 sts, dc2tog, ch 3, sk next ch-3 sp, dc2tog, dc in each of next 3 sts, dc2tog, ch 3, sk next ch, dc in next ch, ch 3, sk next ch, dc2tog, dc in each of next 3 sts, dc2tog, ch 3, sk next ch-3 sp, dc2tog, dc in next st, dc2tog, ch 3, sk next ch-3 sp, dc 3 times in next st, ch 3, sk next ch-3 sp, dc2tog, dc in next st, dc2tog, ch 3, sk next ch-3 sp, [(dc2tog, dc in each of next 3 sts, dc2tog, ch 3, sk next ch, dc in next ch, ch 3, sk next ch, dc2tog, dc in each of next 3 sts, dc2tog, ch 3, sk next ch-3 sp) twice, dc2tog, dc in next st, dc2tog, ch 3, sk next ch-3 sp, dc 3 times in next st, ch 3, sk next ch-3 sp, dc2tog, dc in next st, dc2tog, ch 3, sk next ch-3 sp] 5 times, ch 3, sk next ch-3 sp, dc2tog, dc in each of next 3 sts, dc2tog, ch 2, sk next ch-2 sp, dc in last st, turn.

Row 39: (First-dc, dc) in first st, ch 2, sk next ch-2 sp, dc2tog, dc in next st, dc2tog, ch 3, sk next ch-3 sp, dc3tog, ch 3, sk next ch-3 sp, dc 3 times in next st, ch 3, sk next st, dc 3 times in next st, ch 3, sk next ch-3 sp, dc3tog, ch 3, sk next ch-3 sp, dc2tog, dc in next st, dc2tog, ch 3, sk next ch-3 sp, dc 3 times in next st, ch 3, sk next ch-3 sp, dc2tog, dc in next st, dc2tog, ch 3, sk next ch-3 sp, [dc2tog, dc in next st, dc2tog, ch 3, sk next ch-3 sp, dc 3 times in next st, ch 3, sk next ch-3 sp, dc2tog, dc in next st, dc2tog, ch 3, sk next ch-3 sp, dc3tog, ch 3, sk next ch-3 sp, dc 3 times in next st, ch 3, sk next st, dc 3 times in next st, ch 3, sk next ch-3 sp, dc3tog, ch 3, sk next ch-3 sp, dc2tog, dc in next st, dc2tog, ch 3, sk next ch-3 sp, dc 3 times in next st, ch 3, sk next ch-3 sp, dc2tog, dc in next st, dc2tog, ch 3, sk next ch-3 sp] 5 times, dc2tog, dc in next st, dc2tog, ch 2, sk next ch-2 sp, dc 2 times in last st, turn.

Cut yarn, leaving tail for weaving in; pull tail through last st made; weave in tail using End Cap Finishing Stitch.

FINISHING

Block all pieces to measurements in schematic on p. 77.

Sew Front Panels to Back Panels: Starting at bottom of garment, use Locking Mattress Stitch to sew a 14 (15, 16, 17.5, 18.5, 19.5, 21, 22)"/35.5 (38, 40.5, 44.5, 47, 49.5, 53.5, 56) cm seam; leave 7 (7.5, 8, 8.5, 9, 9.5, 10, 10.5)"/18 (19, 20.5, 21.5, 23, 24, 25.5, 26.5) cm for armhole openings; thread yarn needle with new yarn and sew a remaining length of Front Panel to Back Panel.

Steam sewn seams to even out.
Weave in all ends.

MAINSAIL WRAP

The mainsail is the principle sail on the mainmast of a sailing vessel. Pretty important! This interpretation of the mainsail quadrilateral will, no doubt, be the mainstay in your wardrobe.

Change up your look by wearing this piece right side up or upside down, pinned in front or open and relaxed. The easy rectangular structure of this piece is simple to make, flattering to wear, and lets the stunning Non-Stick Lace and Cables pattern stitch shine through, creating a real showstopper!

SKILL LEVEL: ■■□□
Experienced

SIZES: S (M, L, XL, 2X, 3X, 4X, 5X)
Sample shown in size small

FINISHED MEASUREMENTS
To Fit Bust: 32 (36, 40, 44, 48, 52, 56, 60)"/81.5 (91.5, 101.5, 112, 122, 132, 142, 152.5) cm
Finished Bust: 36 (40.25, 44.25, 48, 52.5, 56.25, 60, 64.5)"/91.5 (102, 112.5, 122, 133.5, 143, 152.5, 164) cm

MATERIALS AND TOOLS

Sample uses Cascade, Venezia Worsted (70% merino wool, 30% silk; 3.5 ounces/100 g = 219 yds/199 m): 6 (6, 7, 8, 8, 9, 10, 10) balls in color Peacock Blue #179—1314 (1314, 1533, 1752, 1752, 1971, 2190, 2190) yards/1202 (1202, 1402, 1603, 1603, 1803, 2003, 2003) m of worsted-weight yarn
Crochet hook: 4.50 mm (size 7) or size to obtain gauge
Yarn needle

BLOCKED GAUGE
Non-Stick Lace and Cables: 4.41 sts = 1"/2.5 cm; 32 sts = 7.25"/18.5 cm; 1.85 rows = 1"/2.5 cm; 12 rows = 6.5"/16.5 cm

Cut yarn, leaving tail for weaving in; pull tail through last st made; weave in tail using End Cap Finishing Stitch.

Left Front

Join yarn same st as last worked tr of Center Back Row 1; first st of Left Front Row 1 worked in same st as joining.

Row 1 (RS): First-tr, [work 2/3 LC] 11 (12, 12, 13, 14, 15, 16, 17) times, tr in next st, turn—57 (62, 62, 67, 72, 77, 82, 87) sts.

Row 2: Ch 1, sc in each st to end of row, turn.

Row 3: First-tr, [yo, (insert hook into next st, yo and pull up a loop to height of first-tr) 5 times (7 loops on hook), yo and draw through 6 loops on hook, yo and draw through remaining 2 loops on hook (sc made), sc 4 times under same 6 loops just worked] 11 (12, 12, 13, 14, 15, 16, 17) times, tr in last st, turn.

Row 4: Rep row 2.

Rows 5–12 (12, 16, 16, 16, 16, 20, 20): Rep last 4 rows.

Sizes S (M, 2X, 3X) Only

Row 13 (13, 17, 17)–15 (15, 19, 19): Rep rows 1–3 once more, turn. Do not cut yarn.

Sizes L (1X, 4X, 5X) Only

Row 17 (17, 21, 21): Rep row 1 once more, turn. Do not cut yarn.

Mainsail Cardi Schematic

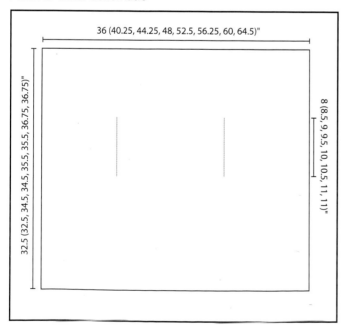

Top of Panel

Next row of Top of Panel re-establishes Non-Stick Lace and Cables pattern st by working sc across Left Front, Back Center, and Right Front panels. Sc2tog decreases are used to close the tops of armholes and return to the pattern as established in the following row.

Transition Row: Ch 1, sc in each of first 55 (60, 60, 65, 70, 75, 80, 85) sts, [sc2tog] twice, sc in each of next 78 (88, 98, 103, 113, 123, 133, 138) sts, [sc2tog] twice, sc in each of next 55 (60, 60, 65, 70, 75, 80, 85) sts, turn—192 (212, 222, 237, 257, 277, 297, 312) sts.

Sizes S (M, 2X, 3X) Only

Rows 1–4: Work in Non-Stick Lace and Cables pattern st.

Sizes L (1X, 4X, 5X) Only

Row 1: Work row 3 of Non-Stick Lace and Cables pattern st.

Row 2: Work row 2 of Non-Stick Lace and Cables pattern st.

Row 3: Work row 1 of Non-Stick Lace and Cables pattern st.

Row 4: Rep row 2.

All Sizes

Rows 5–12: Rep rows 1–4.

Rows 13–14: Rep rows 1 and 2 once more.

Cut yarn, leaving tail for weaving in; pull tail through last st made; weave in tail using End Cap Finishing Stitch.

FINISHING

Block all pieces to measurements in schematic.
Weave in all ends.

TWO CIRCLES WRAP

What could be more perfect than a circle? How about two circles? We've combined two overlapping circles that work together perfectly to create a finished wrap top that is light and easy to wear while adding just a touch of drama to any look. Graceful curves and a flattering open neckline can be adjusted to a custom fit to complement any body.

SKILL LEVEL: ◖■□◗
Easy

SIZES: S (M, L, XL, 2X, 3X, 4X, 5X)
Sample shown in size small

FINISHED MEASUREMENTS
To Fit Bust: 32 (36, 40, 44, 48, 52, 56, 60)"/81.5 (91.5, 101.5, 112, 122, 132, 142, 152.5) cm
Armhole Circumference: 14 (15, 16.75, 18, 19.25, 20.5, 21.5, 22)"/35.5 (38, 42.5, 45.5, 49, 52, 54.5, 56) cm

MATERIALS AND TOOLS

Sample uses Malabrigo, Arroyo (100% superwash merino; 3.53 ounce/100 g = 335 yards/305 m): 2 (2, 2, 2, 2, 3, 3, 3) skeins in color Borraja #AR058—670 (670, 670, 670, 670, 1005, 1005, 1005) yards/613 (613, 613, 613, 613, 919, 919, 919) m of lightweight yarn
Crochet hook: 4.50 mm (size 7) or size to obtain gauge
Yarn needle
Shown using 3, 1" Floral Relief Pedestal Buttons by JUL Designs

BLOCKED GAUGE
Single crochet V-stitch in the round: 3.82 sts = 1"/2.5 cm; 60 sts = 15.71"/40 cm in circumference; 3.25 rounds = 1"/2.5 cm; 26 rounds = 8"/20.5 cm

STITCH GUIDE

Foundation single crochet (Fsc): Ch 2, insert hook in 2nd ch from hook, yo and draw up a loop, yo and draw through 1 loop (first "chain" made), yo and draw through 2 loops on hook (first Fsc made), *insert hook under 2 loops of the "chain" just made, yo and draw up a loop, yo and draw through 1 loop ("chain" made), yo and draw through 2 loops on hook (Fsc made); rep from * for indicated number of foundation sts.

Single crochet V-stitch (Sc-V): (Sc, ch 2, sc) in indicated st or sp.

PATTERN STITCH

Single crochet V-stitch in the round (Sc-V in the rnd) (worked on a multiple of 2 sts)

Swatch: 30 sts and 9 rounds (+1 Fsc round)

Foundation Rnd: Work 30 Fsc, rnd will be joined by making first st of rnd 1 in first Fsc made.

Rnd 1: Sc-V in first st, sk next st, *Sc-V in next st, sk next st; rep from * to end of rnd, join rnd with sl st in first sc of first Sc-V made.

Rnds 2 and 3: Ch 1, Sc-V in ch-2 sp of first Sc-V, Sc-V in ch-2 sp of next Sc-V and in ch-2 sp of each Sc-V to end of rnd, join rnd with sl st in first Sc-V made.

Rnds 4–6: Ch 1, Sc-V in ch-2 sp of first Sc-V, ch 1, *Sc-V in ch-2 sp of next Sc-V, ch 1; rep from * to end of rnd, join rnd with sl st in first Sc-V made.

Rnd 7: Ch 1, Sc-V in ch-2 sp of first Sc-V, ch 2, sk next ch sp, *Sc-V in ch-2 sp of next Sc-V, ch 2, sk next ch sp; rep from * to end of rnd, join rnd with sl st in first Sc-V made.

Rnds 8 and 9: Ch 1, Sc-V in ch-2 sp of first Sc-V, ch 3, sk next ch sp, *Sc-V in ch-2 sp of next Sc-V, ch 3, sk next ch sp; rep from * to end of rnd, join rnd with sl st in first Sc-V made.

Cut yarn and pull through last st made. Join rnd with Duplicate Stitch.

Blocked swatch measurements: 30 Fsc = approximately 7.85"/20 cm circumference; 9 rounds = approximately 2.75"/7 cm

SPECIAL TECHNIQUES

Knotless Starting Chain (see Special Techniques, p. 103)
Duplicate Stitch (see Special Techniques, p. 105)

NOTE

Garment is worked in two pieces worked in the round, then overlapping sections are sewn together after blocking.

INSTRUCTIONS

Body Panel (make 2)

Foundation Rnd: Work 54 (58, 64, 68, 74, 78, 82, 84) Fsc, rnd will be joined by making first st of rnd 1 in first Fsc made.

Be careful not to twist the Foundation rnd when joining. Use Duplicate Stitch with starting yarn tail to join bottom of first Fsc st to bottom of last Fsc st made.

Rnds 1–9: Work in Sc-V in the rnd pattern st.

Rnd 10: Ch 1, Sc-V in ch-2 sp of first Sc-V, Sc-V in next ch sp, *Sc-V in ch-2 sp of next Sc-V, Sc-V in next ch sp; rep from * to end of rnd, join rnd with sl st in first sc of first Sc-V made.

Rnds 11–13: Rep rnd 2.

Rnds 14–17: Rep rnd 4.

Rnds 18–21: Rep rnd 7.

Rnds 22–25: Rep rnd 8.

Size S Only

Rnd 26: Rep rnd 8. Do not join end of rnd with sl st. Cut yarn, leaving tail for weaving in; weave in tail using Duplicate Stitch.

Size M (L, 1X, 2X, 3X, 4X, 5X) Only

Rnd 26: Rep rnd 8.

Rnd 27: Rep rnd 10.

Rnd 28: Rep rnd 2.

Size M Only

Rnd 29: Rep rnd 2. Do not join end of rnd with sl st. Cut yarn, leaving tail for weaving in; weave in tail using Duplicate Stitch.

Size L (1X, 2X, 3X, 4X, 5X) Only

Rnds 29 and 30: Rep rnd 2.

Size L Only

Rnd 31: Rep rnd 4. Do not join end of rnd with sl st. Cut yarn, leaving tail for weaving in; weave in tail using Duplicate Stitch.

Size 1X (2X, 3X, 4X, 5X) Only

Rnds 31–33: Rep rnd 4.

Sc-V in the Rnd

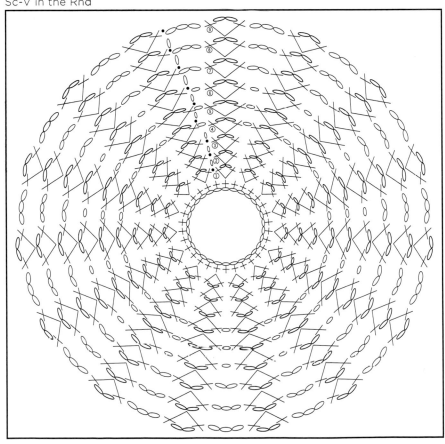

Size 1X Only

Rnd 34: Rep rnd 4. Do not join end of rnd with sl st. Cut yarn, leaving tail for weaving in; weave in tail using Duplicate Stitch.

Size 2X (3X, 4X, 5X) Only

Rnd 34: Rep rnd 4.

Rnds 35 and 36: Rep rnd 7.

Size 2X Only

Rnd 37: Rep rnd 7. Do not join end of rnd with sl st. Cut yarn, leaving tail for weaving in; weave in tail using Duplicate Stitch.

Size 3X (4X, 5X) Only

Rnds 37 and 38: Rep rnd 7.

Rnd 39: Rep rnd 8.

Size 3X Only

Rnd 40: Rep rnd 8. Do not join end of rnd with sl st. Cut yarn, leaving tail for weaving in; weave in tail using Duplicate Stitch.

Size 4X (5X) Only

Rnds 40 and 41: Rep rnd 8.

Size 4X Only

Rnd 42: Rep rnd 8. Do not join end of rnd with sl st. Cut yarn, leaving tail for weaving in; weave in tail using Duplicate Stitch.

Size 5X Only

Rnds 42 and 43: Rep rnd 8.

Rnd 44: Rep rnd 10.

Rnd 45: Rep rnd 2. Do not join rnd with sl st. Cut yarn, leaving tail for weaving in; weave in tail using Duplicate Stitch.

FINISHING

Block to measurements in schematic, making sure to not block armholes too large to ensure snug but comfortable fit.

Lay Body Panels so circles overlap, leaving approximately 14.5 (16, 16.5, 17.5, 18, 18, 18.5, 18.5)"/37 (40.5, 42, 44.5, 45.5, 47, 47) cm between armholes. This distance can be adjusted slightly to provide custom fit. For best fit, pin overlapping circles in place and try on, then adjust overlapping distance if desired.

Sew Body Panels together by first sewing overlapping top panel to underlying panel through overlapping Sc-V st. Next, turn work over and sew overlapping top panel to underlying panel through overlapping Sc-V st.
Gently steam sewn seams, if needed.
Weave in all ends.

Two Circles Wrap Schematic and Assembly

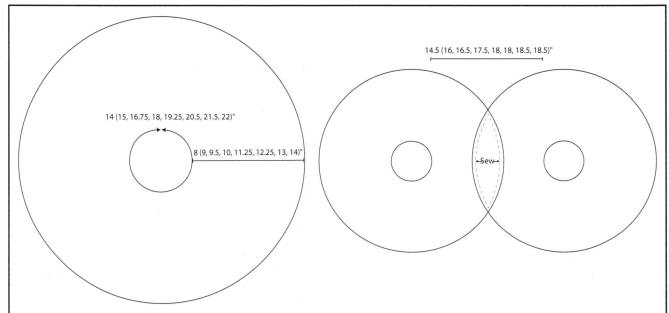

14 (15, 16.75, 18, 19.25, 20.5, 21.5, 22)"

8 (9, 9.5, 10, 11.25, 12.25, 13, 14)"

14.5 (16, 16.5, 17.5, 18, 18, 18.5, 18.5)"

←Sew→

MACRAMÉ LOOK VEST

Inspired by the play of the positive and negative geometric space of macramé, this vest is composed of a series of rectangles pieced together to form a cool, funky vest that reflects your free-spirited nature. Make it as is or add some fringe to hit the market or the next summer music festival in boho-chic style.

SKILL LEVEL: ◖■■■◗
Intermediate

SIZES: S (M, L, XL, 2X, 3X, 4X, 5X)
Sample shown in size small

FINISHED MEASUREMENTS
To Fit Bust: 32 (36, 40, 44, 48, 52, 56, 60)"/81.5 (91.5, 101.5, 112, 122, 132, 142, 152.5) cm
Finished Length from Shoulder: 15.75 (15.75, 19.5, 19.5, 19.5, 23.3, 23.3, 23.3)"/40 (40, 49.5, 49.5, 49.5, 59, 59, 59) cm

MATERIALS AND TOOLS

Sample uses Malabrigo, Sock (100% superwash merino wool; 3.5 ounces/100 g = 440 yards/402 m): 2 (3, 3, 3, 3, 4, 4, 4) hanks in color Terracotta #802—880 (1320, 1320, 1320, 1320, 1760, 1760, 1760) yards/ 805 (1208, 1208, 1208, 1208, 1610, 1610, 1610) m of superfine-weight yarn
Crochet hook: 2.75 mm (size C-2) or size to obtain gauge
Yarn needle

BLOCKED GAUGES
Starburst stitch: 5.58 sts = 1"/2.5 cm; 67 sts = 12"/30.5 cm; 3.57 rows = 1"/2.5 cm;25 rows = 7"/18 cm
Extended single crochet linen stitch: 6.36 sts = 1"/2.5 cm; 35 sts = 5.5"/14 cm; 3.79 rows = 1"/2.5 cm; 18 rows = 4.75"/12 cm
Single crochet linen stitch: 7.37 sts = 1"/2.5 cm; 35 sts = 4.75"/12 cm; 6.67 rows = 1"/2.5 cm; 25 rows = 3.75"/9.5 cm

STITCH GUIDE

Foundation single crochet (Fsc): Ch 2, insert hook in 2nd ch from hook, yo and draw up a loop, yo and draw through 1 loop (first "chain" made), yo and draw through 2 loops on hook (first Fsc made), *insert hook under 2 loops of the "chain" just made, yo and draw up a loop, yo and draw through 1 loop ("chain" made), yo and draw through 2 loops on hook (Fsc made); rep from * for indicated number of foundation sts.

Extended single crochet (ext-sc): Insert hook in next st, yo and draw up a loop, yo and draw through 1 loop on hook, yo and draw through 2 loops on hook.

PATTERN STITCHES

Starburst Stitch (worked on a multiple of 21 + 4 sts)

Swatch: 46 sts and 25 rows (+1 Fsc row)

Foundation Row: Work 46 Fsc, turn.

Row 1 (RS): Ch 1, hdc 2 times in first st, *[ch 1, sk next 2 sts, hdc 3 times in next st] 3 times, ch 7, sk next 5 sts, hdc 3 times in next st, [ch 1, sk next 2 sts, hdc 3 times in next st] twice; rep from * to last 3 sts, ch 1, sk next 2 sts, hdc 2 times in last st, turn.

Row 2: Ch 1, hdc in first st, ch 1, hdc 3 times in next ch-1 sp, *[ch 1, hdc 3 times in next ch-1 sp] twice, ch 4, sc in next ch-7 sp, ch 4, hdc 3 times in next ch-1 sp, [ch 1, hdc 3 times in next ch-1 sp] twice; rep from * to last st, ch 1, hdc in last st, turn.

Row 3: Ch 1, hdc 2 times in first st, *[ch 1, hdc 3 times in next ch-1 sp] twice, ch 4, sc in next ch-4 sp, sc in next st, sc in next ch-4 sp, ch 4, hdc 3 times in next ch-1 sp, ch 1, hdc 3 times in next ch-1 sp; rep from * to last st, ch 1, hdc 2 times in last st, turn.

Row 4: Ch 1, hdc in first st, ch 1, hdc 3 times in next ch-1 sp, *ch 1, hdc 3 times in next ch-1 sp, ch 4, sc in next ch-4 sp, sc in each of next 3 sts, sc in next ch-4 sp, ch 4, hdc 3 times in next ch-1 sp, ch 1, hdc 3 times in next ch-1 sp; rep from * to last st, ch 1, hdc in last st, turn.

Row 5: Ch 1, hdc 2 times in first st, *ch 1, hdc 3 times in next ch-1 sp, ch 4, sc in next ch-4 sp, sc in each of next 5 sts, sc in next ch-4 sp, ch 4, hdc 3 times in next ch-1 sp; rep from * to last st, ch 1, hdc 2 times in last st, turn.

Row 6: Ch 1, hdc in first st, ch 1, hdc 3 times in next ch-1 sp, *ch 5, sc in next ch-4 sp, sc in each of next 7 sts, sc in next ch-4 sp, ch 5, hdc 3 times in next ch-1 sp; rep from * to last st, ch 1, hdc in last st, turn.

Row 7: Ch 1, hdc 2 times in first st, *ch 1, hdc 3 times in next ch-5 sp, ch 4, sk next st, sc in each of next 7 sts, ch 4, hdc 3 times in next ch-5 sp; rep from * to last st, ch 1, hdc 2 times in last st, turn.

Row 8: Ch 1, hdc in first st, ch 1, hdc 3 times in next ch-1 sp, *ch 1, hdc 3 times in next ch-4 sp, ch 4, sk next st, sc in each of next 5 sts, ch 4, hdc 3 times in next ch-4 sp, ch 1, hdc 3 times in next ch-1 sp; rep from * to last st, ch 1, hdc in last st, turn.

Row 9: Ch 1, hdc 2 times in first st, *ch 1, hdc 3 times in next ch-1 sp, ch 1, hdc 3 times in next ch-4 sp, ch 4, sk next st, sc in each of next 3 sts, ch 4, hdc 3 times in next ch-4 sp, ch 1, hdc 3 times in next ch-1 sp; rep from * to last st, ch 1, hdc 2 times in last st, turn.

Row 10: Ch 1, hdc in first st, ch 1, hdc 3 times in next ch-1 sp, *ch 1, hdc 3 times in next ch-1 sp, ch 1, hdc 3 times in next ch-4 sp, ch 4, sk next st, sc in next st, ch 4, hdc 3 times in next ch-4 sp, [ch 1, hdc in next ch-1 sp] twice; rep from * to last st, ch 1, hdc in last st, turn.

Starburst Stitch

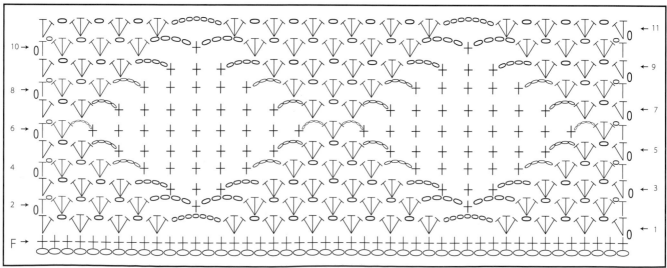

Row 11: Ch 1, hdc 2 times in first st, *[ch 1, hdc 3 times in next ch-1 sp] twice, ch 1, hdc 3 times in next ch-4 sp, ch 7, hdc 3 times in next ch-4 sp, [ch 1, hdc 3 times in next ch-1 sp] twice; rep from * to last st, ch 1, hdc 2 times in last st, turn.

Rep rows 2–11 for pattern st.

Single crochet linen stitch (sc linen st) (worked on a multiple of 2 + 1 sts)

Swatch: 35 sts and 25 rows (+1 Fsc row)

Foundation Row: Work 35 Fsc, turn.

Row 1: Ch 1, sc in first st, *ch 1, sk next st, sc in next st; rep from * to end of row, turn.

Row 2: Ch 1, sc in first st, *sc in next ch-1 sp, ch 1, sk next sc; rep from * to last ch-1 sp, sc in last ch-1 sp, sc in last st, turn.

Row 3: Ch 1, sc in first st, *ch 1, sk next st, sc in next ch-1 sp; rep from * to last 2 sts, ch 1, sk next st, sc in last st, turn.

Rep rows 2 and 3 for pattern st.

Extended single crochet linen stitch (ext-sc linen st) (worked on a multiple of 2 + 1 sts)

Swatch: 35 sts and 18 rows (+1 Fsc row)

Foundation Row: Work 35 Fsc, turn.

Row 1: Ch 1, ext-sc in first st, *ch 1, sk next st, ext-sc in next st; rep from * to end of row, turn.

Row 2: Ch 1, ext-sc in first st, *ext-sc in next ch-1 sp, ch 1, sk next ext-sc; rep from * to last ch-1 sp, ext-sc in last ch-1 sp, ext-sc in last st, turn.

Row 3: Ch 1, ext-sc in first st, *ch 1, sk next st, ext-sc in next ch-1 sp; rep from * to last 2 sts, ch 1, sk next st, ext-sc in last st, turn.

Rep rows 2 and 3 for pattern st.

SPECIAL TECHNIQUES

Knotless Starting Chain (see Special Techniques, p. 103)
End Cap Finishing Stitch (see Special Techniques, p. 108)
Locking Mattress Stitch (see Special Techniques, p. 104)

NOTES

1. Garment is made from the center out to the sleeves, then front panels are made separately.

2. Left Side and Right Side refer to left and right side as worn.

3. When instructed to work in a pattern stitch "as established," work the next row of pattern and ensure that the stitches line up as in previous rows.

Sc linen st

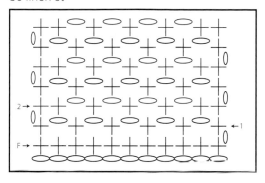

Ext-sc linen st

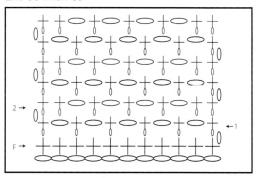

INSTRUCTIONS

First Half of Back

Foundation Row: Work 88 (88, 109, 109, 109, 130, 130, 130) Fsc, turn.

Rows 1–27 (30, 34, 37, 44, 45, 48, 52): Work in Starburst Stitch pattern st.

Cut yarn, leaving tail for weaving in; pull tail through last st made; weave in tail using End Cap Finishing Stitch.

Second Half of Back

With RS facing, join yarn in bottom of first st of Foundation Row; first st of row 1 is made in same st as joining.

Work as for First Half of Back. (In other words, do exactly the same thing you did to make the first half of the back you just made!)

Front Panel (make 2)

Foundation Row: Work 88 (88, 109, 109, 109, 130, 130, 130) Fsc, turn.

Rows 1–55 (57, 65, 75, 77, 87, 95, 97): Work in Starburst Stitch pattern st.

Begin Front Border

NOTE: When working Transition Row, sc in each of the ch of the ch-4 sps and in each of the hdc but not in the ch-1 sps between the "hdc 3" groups.

Transition Row: Ch 1, sc in each of first 3 sts, [sc 2 times in next st, sc in each of next 2 sts] 28 (28, 35, 35, 35, 42, 42, 42) times, sc 2 times in next st, turn—117 (117, 145, 145, 145, 173, 173, 173) sts.

Rows 1–10: Work in sc linen st.

Cut yarn, leaving tail for weaving in; pull tail through last st made; weave in tail using End Cap Finishing Stitch.

Side Panel (make 2)

Foundation Row: Work 19 Fsc, turn.

Rows 1–39 (37, 36, 34, 48, 46, 44, 42): Work in ext-sc linen st.

Cut yarn, leaving tail for weaving in; pull tail through last st made; weave in tail using End Cap Finishing Stitch.

FINISHING

Block all pieces to measurements in schematic.
Using Locking Mattress Stitch, sew seams as follows:
Sew Side Panels to either side of Back Panel.
Sew Front Panels to Side Panels.
Sew 4 (5, 6, 7, 8, 9, 10, 11)"/10 (12.5, 15, 18, 20.5, 23, 25.5, 28) cm shoulder seam.
Gently block seams to even out, if needed.
Weave in all ends.

Macramé Look Vest Schematic

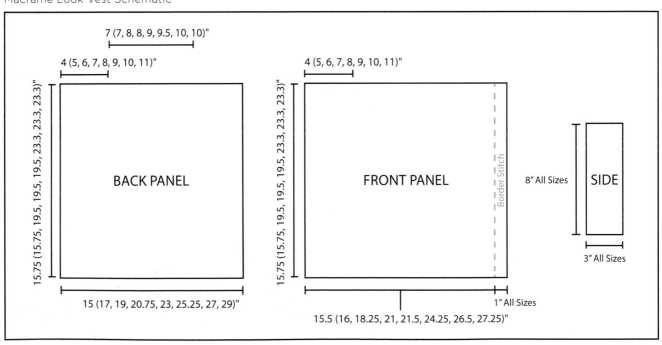

SPECIAL TECHNIQUES

IN THIS SECTION, YOU WILL FIND WRITTEN INSTRUCTIONS AND PHOTO TUTORIALS FOR THE STITCHES AND TECHNIQUES USED MOST COMMONLY THROUGHOUT THIS BOOK. WE HAVE USED CONTRASTING COLORS FOR THE TECHNIQUES IN THIS SECTION TO MAKE IT EASIER FOR YOU TO SEE THE STITCHES.

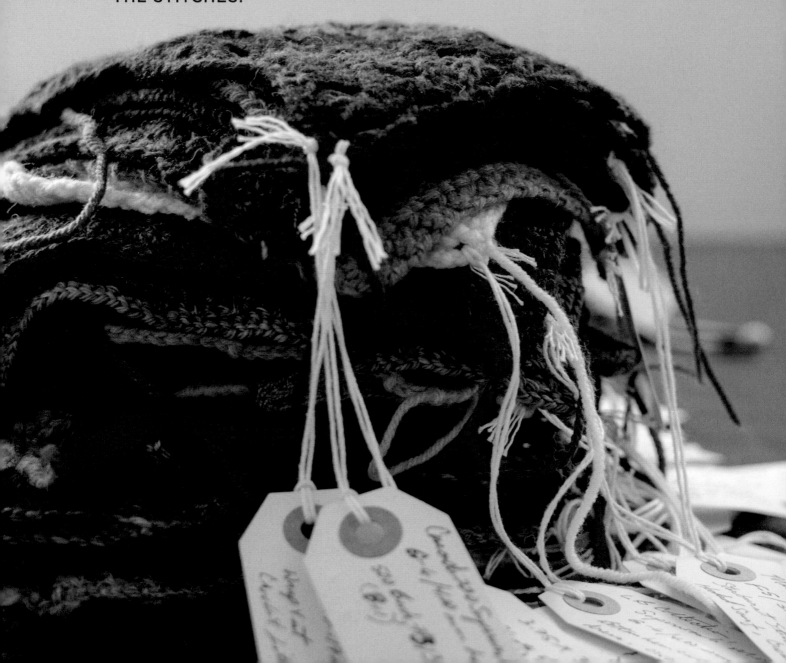

KNOTLESS STARTING CHAIN

1. Pass the tail of the yarn from back to front over your hook crossing the tail in front of your working yarn (the yarn coming from the ball or skein). Firmly hold the crossing point where the tail and working yarn cross.
2. Yarn over and draw up a loop, being careful to maintain a firm hold on the crossing point.
3. Chain 1 for first st.
4. Insert hook back into the Knotless Starting Chain so the crossing point is on the top of the hook.
5. Make stitches as indicated in pattern (Fsc row shown here).
6. Close loop by firmly grasping the starting tail with one hand while holding work with other hand.
7. Gently pull tail until loop from Knotless Starting Chain disappears into the row, being careful to match tension of neighboring loops.

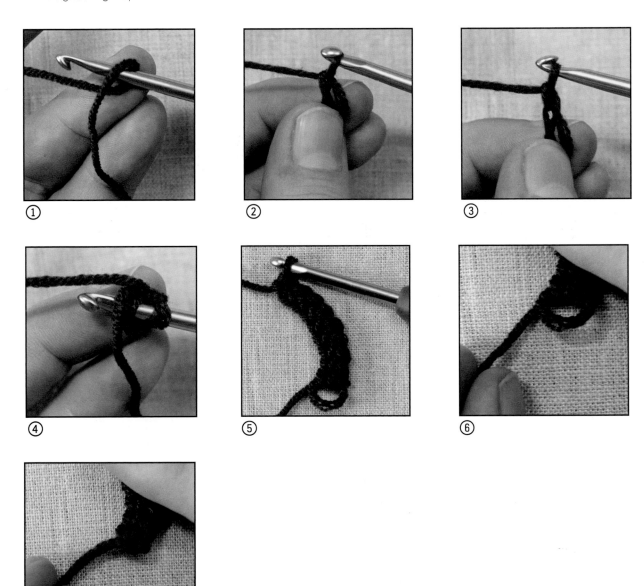

LOCKING MATTRESS STITCH

Begin by laying work with RS down and edges to be sewn side by side. Stitches will be worked through the top loop only of both sides.

1. First, insert needle from left to right through first stitches of both panels at the bottom of your work to begin joining the two panels.
2. Next, moving up the seam, insert needle from right to left through next loop on the right panel and continue by inserting the needle through the last loop worked of the left panel.
3. Next, again moving up the seam, insert needle from left to right through next loop on the left panel and continue by inserting the needle through the last loop worked of the right panel.
4. Continue in this manner, repeating steps 2 and 3; gently pull yarn snug as you go to close the seam, being careful to match the fabric gauge so as to not create a puckered seam.

②

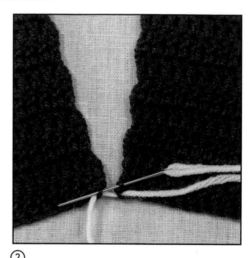
③

①

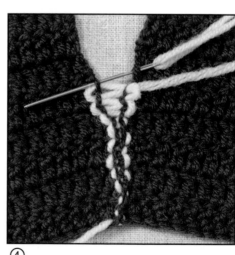
④

DUPLICATE STITCH

Work last stitch of round and cut yarn leaving about a 6-10"/15-25 cm tail.

1. Draw last loop still on hook all the way through last stitch made until tail passes through stitch. Thread tail through yarn needle.
2. Skip next stitch (first stitch of round). With yarn needle, run end of tail under both loops of next stitch and pull yarn through.
3. Insert needle back through where tail originally came from (last stitch made) and behind work.
4. Snug yarn to cover skipped stitch with duplicate stitch just made matching tension of other stitches.
5. Working from back of stitches, bring yarn up through center of duplicate stitch just made *and* underlying stitch.
6. Skip next stitch. Run end of tail under both loops of next stitch and pull yarn through.
7. Insert needle back through where tail originally came from (duplicate stitch *and* underlying stitch).
8. Snug yarn to cover skipped stitch with duplicate stitch just made matching tension of other stitches. Weave in tail.

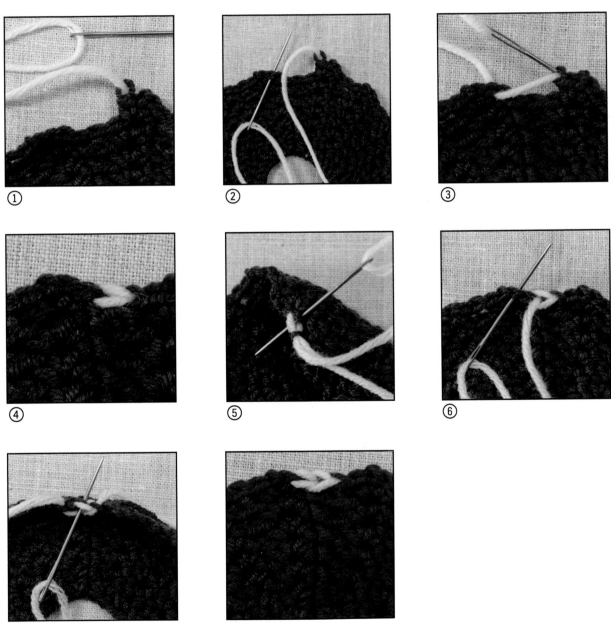

FOUNDATION SINGLE CROCHET

1. Chain 2, insert hook in 2nd chain from hook, yarn over and draw up a loop.
2. Yarn over and draw through 1 loop (first "chain" made).
3. Yarn over and draw through 2 loops on hook (first foundation single crochet made).
4. Insert hook under 2 loops of the "chain" just made.
5. Yarn over and draw up a loop.
6. Yarn over and draw through 1 loop ("chain" made).
7. Yarn over and draw through 2 loops on hook (foundation single crochet made).
8. Repeat steps 4–7 for indicated number of foundation stitches.

FOUNDATION DOUBLE CROCHET

1. Chain 2, insert hook in 2nd chain from hook, yarn over and draw up a loop.
2. Yarn over and draw through 1 loop (first "chain" made).
3. Yarn over and draw through 2 loops on hook.
4. Chain 2 (first foundation double crochet made).
5. Yarn over and insert hook under 2 loops of "chain" just made.
6. Yarn over and draw up a loop.
7. Yarn over and draw through 1 loop ("chain" made).
8. (Yarn over and draw through 2 loops on hook) twice (foundation double crochet made).
9. Repeat steps 5–8 for indicated number of foundation stitches.

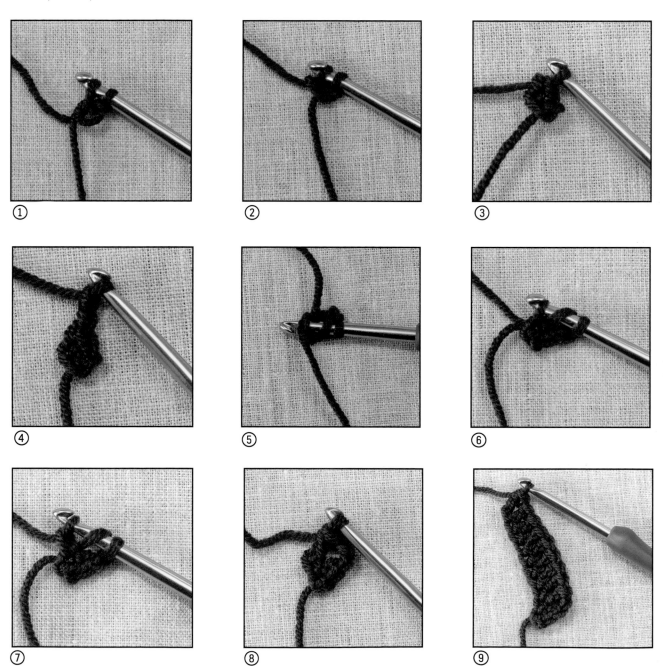

① ② ③
④ ⑤ ⑥
⑦ ⑧ ⑨

END CAP FINISHING STITCH

Technique shown using double crochet stitch.

1. Work last stitch of row and cut yarn leaving about a 6-10"/15-25 cm tail.
2. Draw last loop still on hook all the way through last stitch made until tail passes through stitch. Thread tail through yarn needle.
3. Insert hook from front to back under two side loops at bottom of last stitch made. Gently pull yarn snug to match tension of other stitches.
4. Insert needle into center of stitch where tail originally came from (last stitch made).
5. Gently pull yarn snug to create a tidy corner being careful to match tension of last stitch made. Weave in remaining tail.

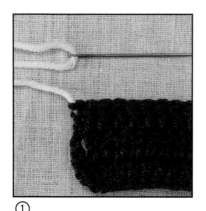
①

②

③

④

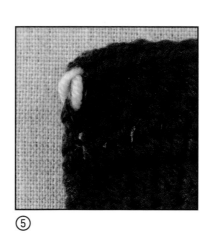
⑤

Acknowledgments

Once again I have come to the end of a major project and I find myself experiencing a feeling of both immense accomplishment and overwhelming gratitude. Every day I get to do the things that I love the most, but I couldn't do any of it without the support and assistance of a FAB team of talented and inspired people.

Susanna Tobias, tech editor: We've grown up together in this industry, and now I've finally have had the honor of working with you on a project. Your exacting precision and attention to detail have made the patterns in this book a thing of beauty, and I can't wait for people to see just how talented you are. Thank you for lending your skills—looking forward to working with you again!

Linda Roghaar, Linda Roghaar Literary Agency: Thank you for your support and encouragement through this stage of my career. I can't begin to tell you how much it means to have such a committed and passionate professional in my corner guiding and pulling for me. You take my work as seriously as I do, and I thank you for it, again.

Connie, Marilyn, Jennifer, and the team at Sterling Publishing: When we sat at that conference table in New York and you all looked at Jason and me and said you believed in us, I think our whole world changed. We both have the utmost respect for you all, and knowing that your energies were behind us as we produced this book made all the difference in the world when it got a little tough. Thank you for your confidence and your faith in us. Let's do it again!

To the AH-MAY-ZING team of adept contract crocheters I have the good fortune of working with: Your talent and passion have helped make the vision of *Crochet Geometry* a reality. Without all of you, I wouldn't be able to make this work, and I am filled with gratitude that the universe has brought you all into my family's life.

Cookie Gates
Cami Peacock
Lara O.
Patrick Lyddy
Catherine Riche

Deborah Meabon
Katherine Frick
LeeAnn Wilson
Juanita Quiñones

To the beautiful models whose faces and bodies grace these pages, showing off these garments with style and panache. It's not easy putting yourself out there; thank you for making it look that way.

Andrea Alder
Barbara R.
Leslie Ann Engen

Julie Cash
Tia McLaughlin

I'm also grateful to these companies for their generous support of yarn and products for the samples in *Crochet Geometry:*

Cascade Yarns
Crystal Palace Yarns
Laura Bellows, JUL Designs
Lion Brand

Malabrigo
Mango Moon
Tahki Stacy Charles

Lastly, and most importantly, I want to acknowledge the driving force behind my work for over twenty years. Jason Mullett-Bowlsby, you have never failed to say "Sure!" and jump on board when I've come up with my next big idea. Once again, at the finish of another of those big ideas, I find myself knowing surely that I could never have brought this project across the finish line without you. Your influence is evident on every page of this book through your photography and graphic work, but it is your influence in my life that I am forever grateful for. Without your love, support, encouragement, talent, and *amazing* cooking, I just couldn't do this. We make a pretty good team, me leading the charge and you making sure I don't charge right off the cliff! You have my respect and all my love, always.

CHART KEY

Chain (ch)

Slip Stitch (sl st)

Single Crochet (sc)

Half Double Crochet (hdc)

Double Crochet (dc)

Treble Crochet (tr)

Double Treble Crochet (dtr)

Foundation Single Crochet (Fsc)

Foundation Double (Fdc)

First Double Crochet (First-dc)

First Treble Crochet (First-tr)

Extended Single Crochet (ext-sc)

3-Double Crochet Fan (3-dc fan):

Double Crochet Fan (dc-fan)

Non-Stick Lace

Single Crochet Through Back Loop Only (Sc-tbl)

Single Crochet Through Front Loop Only (Sc-tfl)

Front Post Cluster (FP-Cl)

Front Post Double Crochet (FPdc)

Back Post Double Crochet (BPdc)

Front Post Treble Crochet (FPtr)

Single Crochet V-stitch (Sc-V)

Double Crochet V-stitch (Dc-V)
As seen in Five Easy Pieces

Double Crochet V-stitch (Dc-V)
As seen in Wrap Front Shrug

Inverted Double Crochet V-stitch (Inverted Dc-V)
Double crochet 2 together (dc2tog)

Double Crochet 3 Together (dc3tog)

Front Post Double Crochet V-stitch (FPdc-V)

Direction of Work

F   Foundation Row

CABLE CHART KEY

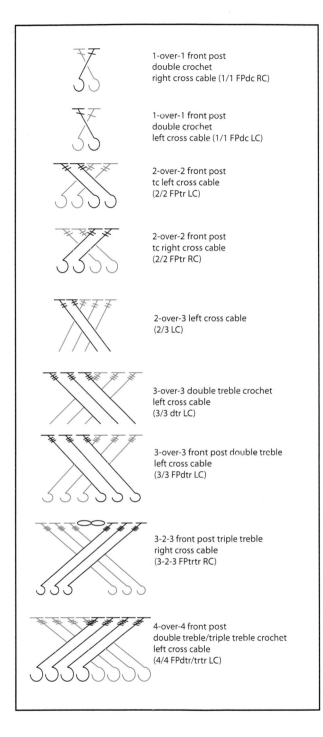

1-over-1 front post
double crochet
right cross cable (1/1 FPdc RC)

1-over-1 front post
double crochet
left cross cable (1/1 FPdc LC)

2-over-2 front post
tc left cross cable
(2/2 FPtr LC)

2-over-2 front post
tc right cross cable
(2/2 FPtr RC)

2-over-3 left cross cable
(2/3 LC)

3-over-3 double treble crochet
left cross cable
(3/3 dtr LC)

3-over-3 front post double treble
left cross cable
(3/3 FPdtr LC)

3-2-3 front post triple treble
right cross cable
(3-2-3 FPtrtr RC)

4-over-4 front post
double treble/triple treble crochet
left cross cable
(4/4 FPdtr/trtr LC)

MATERIALS

Circle T-top
Malabrigo, Sock
http://www.malabrigoyarns.com

Cocoon Shrug
Lion Brand, Wool-Ease
http://www.lionbrand.com

Cowl Neck Tunic
Cascade Yarns, Heritage Sock
http://www.cascadeyarns.com

Five Easy Pieces
Lion Brand Collection, Superwash Merino
http://www.lionbrand.com

Gathered Shoulder Sleeveless Top
Mango Moon Yarns, Mulberry Meadow
http://www.mangomoonyarns.com

Half Circle Cardigan
Tahki Stacy Charles, Cotton Classic Lite
http://www.tahkistacycharles.com

Macramé Look Vest
Malabrigo, Sock
http://www.malabrigoyarns.com

Mainsail Wrap
Cascade Yarns, Venezia Worsted
http://www.cascadeyarns.com

Rectangles Top
Malabrigo, Rios
http://www.malabrigoyarns.com

Shawl Collar Cardi
Cascade Yarns, Heritage 150
http://www.cascadeyarns.com

Sleeve Shrug
Lion Brand Collection, Superwash Merino
http://www.lionbrand.com

Split Circle Wrap
Cascade Yarns, Longwood Sport
http://www.cascadeyarns.com

T-top
Malabrigo, Sock
http://www.malabrigoyarns.com

Two Circles Wrap
Malabrigo, Arroyo
http://www.malabrigoyarns.com

Wrap Front Shrug
Crystal Palace Yarns, Panda Silk
http://www.traw.com

**All fasteners and attachments provided by Laura Bellows
of JUL Designs**
http://www.juldesigns.com

About the Designer and Photographer

Shannon and Jason are the DIY duo known as the Shibaguyz behind the design studios of Shibaguyz Designz, a versatile design company that uses their unique flair to combine fashion design, knitting, crochet, photography, and graphic design into a cohesive whole.

Shannon's award-winning crochet and knit designs have been featured in and on the covers of both US and international publications. He currently has over 200 published patterns credited to his name since his first design was featured on the cover of a magazine in 2010. Shannon has been teaching adults for twenty-plus years and is a Craft Yarn Council certified instructor. His quirky sense of humor and relatable teaching style have made him a sought-after teacher in both local and national venues.

You can find Shannon's designs in countless magazines such as *Crochet!* and *Noro Knitting Magazine*, or in one of his many books including *Designer Crochet: 32 Patterns to Elevate Your Style* also available from Lark Crafts.

Jason is a professional fashion and portrait photographer whose photography can be seen in many of the Shibaguyz's pattern books. Jason also works as a freelance book-packaging designer and photographer for indie knitwear designers as well as major publishing houses like Lark Crafts, Leisure Arts, Quayside, and Creative Publishing.

Even though Jason loves his work in fashion and portrait photography, his work with four-legged models is some of his most "ooooh" and "ahhhh" inducing work.

Shannon and Jason live in Seattle, Washington, with their three Shiba Inu, the Shibakidz, who, more or less, support their ventures as long as enough time is taken for walks and treats.

Index

Note: Page numbers in *italics* indicate projects.

A

Abbreviations and lingo, XII–XIV

B

Blocked gauge, about, X–XI. *See also specific projects*
Blocking, about, XI
Book overview, IV–VII

C

Cable Chart Key, 111
Cardigans, 17–44
    Five Easy Pieces, *19–27*, 111
    Half Circle Cardigan, *37–44*, 111
    Shawl Collar Cardigan, *29–35*, 111
Chart Keys, 110–111
Circle T-top, *51–55*, 111
Cocoon Shrug, *9–11*, 111
Conversion table, US to UK, XIV
Cowl Neck Tunic, *67–70*, 111

D

Double crochet, foundation, 107
Duplicate Stitch, 105

E

Easy projects
    about: description of, VIII
    Cowl Neck Tunic, *67–70*, 111
    Gathered Shoulder Sleeveless Top, *63–65*, 111
    Rectangles Top, *57–61*, 111
    Shawl Collar Cardigan, *29–35*, 111
    Two Circles Wrap, *91–95*, 111
End Cap Finishing Stitch, 108
Experienced projects
    about: description of, VIII
    Five Easy Pieces (cardigan), *19–27*, 111
    Mainsail Wrap, *85–89*, 111
    Sleeve Shrug, *3–7*, 111
    Split Circle Wrap, *73–83*, 111
    T-top, *45–49*, 111

F

Fasteners, source for, 111
Finishing stitch, end cap, 108
Five Easy Pieces (cardigan), *19–27*, 111
Foundation Double Crochet, 107
Foundation Single Crochet, 106

G

Gathered Shoulder Sleeveless Top, *63–65*, 111
Gauge, blocked, X–XI

H

Half Circle Cardigan, *37–44*, 111

I

Intermediate projects
    about: description of, VIII
    Circle T-top, *51–55*, 111
    Cocoon Shrug, *9–11*, 111
    Half Circle Cardigan, *37–44*, 111
    Macramé Look Vest, *97–101*, 111
    Wrap Front Shrug, *13–16*, 111

K

Knotless Starting Chain, 103

L

Locking Mattress Stitch, 104

M

Macramé Look Vest, *97–101*, 111
Mainsail Wrap, *85–89*, 111
Materials sources, 111
Mattress stitch, locking, 104

P

Projects. *See also* Cardigans; Pullovers; Shrugs; Wraps
    abbreviations and lingo, XII–XIV
    blocked gauge, X–XI
    blocking, XI
    design creation, IV–V
    difficulty levels explained, VIII. *See also specific levels*
    getting started, VIII–XIV
    making, VI
    making gauge swatch, XI
    materials sources, 111
    reading patterns, VI
    seeing, VI
    success tips, V–VII
    wearing, VII
    yarn selection, IX–X
Pullovers, 45–70
    Circle T-top, *51–55*, 111
    Cowl Neck Tunic, *67–70*, 111

Pullovers *(continued)*
    Gathered Shoulder Sleeveless Top,
      63–65, 111
    Rectangles Top, *57–61*, 111
    T-top, *45–49*, 111

R
Rectangles Top, *57–61*, 111
Resources
    Abbreviations chart, XIV
    Cable Chart Key, 110
    Chart Key, 110
    materials sources, 111
    project skill levels, VIII
    special techniques. *See* Stitches and
      special techniques
    US to UK Conversion Table, XIV

S
Shawl Collar Cardigan, *29–35*, 111
Shrugs, 1–16
    Cocoon Shrug, *9–11*, 111
    Sleeve Shrug, *3–7*, 111
    Wrap Front Shrug, *13–16*, 111
Single crochet, foundation, 106
Sleeve Shrug, *3–7*, 111
Sources, for materials, 111
Special techniques. *See* Stitches
  and special techniques
Split Circle Wrap, *73–83*, 111
Stitches and special techniques
    Abbreviations chart, XIV
    Duplicate Stitch, 105
    End Cap Finishing Stitch, 108
    Foundation Double Crochet, 107
    Foundation Single Crochet, 106
    Knotless Starting Chain, 103
    Locking Mattress Stitch, 104
    US to UK Conversion Table, XIV
Stitch guide, about, XII
Swatch, making gauge, XI

T
Techniques. *See* Stitches and
  special techniques
Tension (blocked gauge), X–XI
T-top, *45–49*, 111
Tunic, cowl neck, *67–70*, 111
Two Circles Wrap, *91–95*, 111

U
US to UK Conversion Table, XIV

V
Vest, macramé look, *97–101*, 111

W
Weight, yarn, IX
Wrap Front Shrug, *13–16*, 111
Wraps, 71–101
    Macramé Look Vest, *97–101*, 111
    Mainsail Wrap, *85–89*, 111
    Split Circle Wrap, *73–83*, 111
    Two Circles Wrap, *91–95*, 111

Y
Yarn
    blocked gauge, X–XI
    content, IX
    selecting for projects, IX–X
    substituting type, IX
    weight, IX